Wyche Way
to Teach

A Miscellany of Teaching and Learning

Geoff Rutherford

Preface

This book has been written in the hope that some of the thoughts held within its pages will add something meaningful to the discussions around Teaching and Learning. It is my contention that the majority of thinking and research that has the capacity to truly enhance children's learning appears counter intuitive on first reading. So whilst I hold to all the views expressed in the book (I wouldn't have written them if I didn't believe them!) I accept that by their very nature, much of the thinking may initially appear to challenge conventional wisdom. I make no apologies for this but trust that those who are gracious enough to take the time to read will also be gracious enough to take time to engage in the debate; using the thoughts expressed here as a springboard to deepen their own thinking

The book's secondary purpose comes out of the school's link with Gofu Juu, a primary school in Tanzania. I first visited the school in 2008, I was struck by the beauty of the country and the all-encompassing warmth of the African welcome. However as we toured the school I was shown into a tiny room where there lay a meagre bowl of a thin white watery liquid that was set aside to feed the 170 orphans. I was informed that the small cup of maize and water mix was likely to be their only meal of the day. Upon returning to the UK the school established a charity called Wychumvi that now feeds every child in the school daily.

It is our hope that this book will make a small contribution to the lives of children in both countries. We trust that the ideas expressed in its pages will impact on the teaching of those who read them, and in so doing enhance children's learning. But just as importantly all the money from the sale of each book will be sent to Gofu Juu to support the many children whose lives have been blighted by Aids and yet have been so enriched by the support and giving of so many in the UK.

Contents

ARE WALT AND WILF REALLY WES IN DISGUISE?
(WES - WASTE OF EDUCATIONAL SPACE)

Despite the title the Wyche is strongly committed to the concept of Learning Objectives but to quote Spock from the Star Trek movie... *"not learning objectives as we know them captain"*

A few years ago there was a great focus on the concept of learning objectives, much of which focused on the excellent work of Shirley Clarke. Her ideas built on the principles outlined by Wiliam and Black in their seminal work *"Inside the Black Box"* which provided groundbreaking research on formative assessment. However, as pedagogy moved from philosophy to implementation, the purity of the original work became increasingly diluted. At their worse learning objectives came to be a sentence lifted from the teacher's planning, placed on the board at the beginning of the lesson for the children to supposedly imbibe, in the vain hope that they would see the learning within the lesson and be more engaged. In truth this practice became little more than educational wallpaper and something to ingratiate oneself to Ofsted inspectors as the received wisdom was that they appeared to value them.

It was the shallowness of implementation and the lack of robust philosophical underpinning that led to The Wyche not to pursue the path of Walts and Wilfs which became common in many schools. It is not that the concepts were wrong but once the DfE got hold of them and turned them into popularist theory the watered down version added little in value to classroom practice. In truth I think it might be fair to say that Shirley Clarke herself sought to distance herself from the simplistic approach adopted by many and called Walt and Wilf "her bastard children" (quote from Barry Hymer –NPH conference June 2012) She herself was clearly perturbed by the failure of those in the DfE to implement the pedagogy effectively.

Having said all that, the school still holds to the belief that the learning objective debate lies at the heart of all good teaching and learning and that rather than throwing out the proverbial baby with the bath water, we should engage with the research and look afresh at the role of learning objectives within the primary curriculum.

For me the original learning objective debate came with two fundamental flaws, one relating to pedagogy and the other relating to what the learning objective should be seeking to achieve. As in all areas of education the key to effective teaching lies in a deep engagement with the principles of learning. The whole concept of teaching and learning is too complex to be reduced to a series of formulaic teaching methods and the roll out of the Walt and Wilf principles were a prime example. The rest of this article looks at these two flaws and shows how; with secure philosophical underpinning they can be redeemed to have a fundamental impact on the teaching and learning within the primary classroom.

The Issue of Pedagogy

The school makes no apology in declaring itself to hold to a "constructivist" theory in its understanding of how children learn. In layman's terms this means that there is a recognition that all learning comes from the child and is constructed within the mind of the child. There may well be a place for a teacher to model certain areas of learning but there is the understanding that it is only the active engagement of the child in constructing their own understanding of a given concept that will lead to effective long term learning.

The introduction of the Learning Objective stated clearly at the beginning of the lesson was often a direct contradiction to this philosophical belief of how children learn. If the Science lesson was designed to explore how materials might be separated then a good teacher might dissolve sugar into a cup of hot water and then ask the children to discuss how they might, or even whether they can, be separated again. If behind the teacher, the learning objective on the board makes clear to the children that the purpose of the lesson is to learn; *"to separate dissolved materials by evaporating the liquid"* then the heart is rather ripped out of any exploration the children may wish to have undertaken within the lesson.

This is not to imply that the concept of the Learning Objective is wrong, as we shall see later in this article a true understanding and appreciation of how they should be used is one of the most fundamental building blocks that a teacher can use in terms of classroom practice. However the ill thought through use of bland objectives dumped on a board indiscriminately and out of a formulaic sense of what is good practice will have a tendency to undermine learning rather than enhance it.

In truth there are some lessons that benefit greatly from having the learning objective clearly articulated to the learner at the outset, but these will be minimal. For most lessons that seek to build learning from within the child the learning objective should be used judiciously. This means that the teacher may choose to present the learning objective to the children at a strategic point in the lesson, this may be to clarify an element of learning that the children have explored, or it may form a plenary at the conclusion of the lesson where the children summarise their learning. Whatever the strategy, teaching is too complex a task to do the same thing, in the same format, within every lesson. Teaching is a craft that comes alive in the hands of those in the profession who appreciate its intricacy and the nuances that draw out the richest learning from children.

The Learning Objective and the Curriculum Objective

The second flaw in the learning objective debate relates to the concept of learning itself. For many the learning objective has become synonymous with statements found in the Numeracy or Literacy Strategy, or the programmes of study from the National Curriculum. It might sound somewhat bizarre to say it, but many of the statements found in these documents don't relate to the learning but seek to flesh out the concept to be acquired at the end of a unit of work. To illustrate this from the Literacy framework; I have seen plenty of lessons where the learning objective for the lesson relates to children using "powerful adjectives". This is a laudable goal, but that is precisely what it is –an end goal. The learning relates to the journey not the destination. So whilst the hope upon concluding a unit of work may well be that the children would be able to write a piece of fictional writing that is greatly enhanced by the use of powerful adjectives, this relates little to the journey the child takes to get there and this is the process of learning. The key question is not where am I heading but how do I get there? The child needs to know what a powerful adjective is; they then need to know how to construct one of their own. These are the elements of the learning that will ultimately deliver the quality of writing.

The danger is that at this point the teacher has not clearly articulated in the mind of the child, nor often even in their own mind what the learning process actually is. The learning then degenerates into a form of osmosis where the teacher reads texts to the children all of which contain "powerful adjectives" and if the children are lucky, or more likely, if they are well read they will be able to imbibe the concept through a general vague assimilation rather than through a process of clear structured learning.

The truth is that teachers need to deconstruct their understanding of what makes a "powerful adjective" so that they can teach it directly and clearly to children. It is only then that the true power of the "learning" objective fully comes into play. So using our example of the powerful adjectives, the teacher may want to explain to the child that "big" is not a powerful adjective because it can be used to describe a myriad of different things from a big chair to a big elephant, it is this which prevents the word being effective in a piece of writing. A powerful adjective is one which can only be used in the fewest number of contexts. Thus "towering castle" is better than "big castle" because the word "towering" can be used in fewer contexts. One might have a towering chair, but the picture one derives form this is a chair with disproportionate leg size. The power comes from the narrowing of the word usage. This is a "learning" objective in its truest form because it provides the child with the information they need to undertake the learning and fulfil the objective set for the unit of work.

To clarify the difference between the objective for the unit of work (the destination) and the learning objective (the journey) the school came up with titles which sought to differentiate the two. The distinction was drawn between a "Curriculum Objective" and a "Learning Objective"

The curriculum objective are those usually taken from the National Curriculum Programmes of Study or the Frameworks for Numeracy or Literacy and invariably relate to what the children will have achieved by the end of the unit of work/lesson. The assessment of these objectives will usually be summative in the sense that they will "test" whether the child has taken on the learning through the lesson/s

Examples of Curriculum Objectives might include:

- "Use units of time (seconds, minutes, hours, days) and know the relationships between them; read the time to the quarter hour; identify time intervals, including those that cross the hour" (Maths Year 2)
- "Clarify meaning and point of view by using varied sentence structure (phrases, clauses and adverbials)" (Literacy Year 4)
- "To recognise how places fit within a wider geographical context (for example, as part of a bigger region or country) and are interdependent (for example, through the supply of goods, movements of people)" (Geography Year 6)

In contrast the Learning Objective will be drawn from the teacher's own engagement with the task and their opinion as to what constitutes the learning in any given activity. The assessment of the task will tend to be more formative than summative especially where the learning is undertaken in a series of stages that ultimately facilitates the full understanding of the concept outlined in the broader curriculum objective. The assessment should also relate tightly to the child's understanding of the learning rather than the outcome of the work.

So again, using the example of the adjectives above, the assessment should explore whether the child understands the principle of what creates a powerful adjective rather than just whether he has used them in his story. It may be that he has understood the concept but for that one lesson cannot find the right word, but this is better than the child who has not grasped the principle behind the learning but just happens to have stumbled across a good word to include in the story through chance. This type of assessment will also enable the teacher to plan further units of work effectively because they can be confident they are building on secure understanding rather than simply a child's ability to complete a given task (whilst always accepting that completing the task may form an integral part of the assessment process of course)

Examples of Learning Objectives might include:

- To understand that time is a measure and how this measure relates to the fact that a clock is divided into quarters (Mathematics Year 2)
- The use of short sentences for dramatic effect and suspense. The fact that short sentences cause the reader to stop. Looking at the associated issue of punctuation. (Literacy Year 4)
- To focus on the impact of the subsidised American banana industry on the lives of the St Lucian farmers. To understand that governmental decisions play a major role in shaping trade and economics. (Geography Year 6)

This approach has taken the staff here on a rich journey of exploring the true nature of the learning in any given lesson. The following are a selection of examples that seek to illustrate the dangers of teaching from curriculum objectives and the consequent power of engaging with the learning as opposed to the outcome.

Example 1: The Right Angle in Year 2
The understanding of True Learning
The Numeracy Strategy (1998) states that "pupils should know a quarter turn is a right angle" The teacher set up a lesson (which to be fair I have seen countless times) where a piece of paper is folded twice to create a "right angle" template and children were then encouraged to move around the classroom exploring shapes they could find that contained "right angles". By the end of the lesson they had a healthy list of objects from the edge of tables to window frames. The learning looked secure except the lesson focused on the "outcome" rather than the "process" and the true learning is in the latter rather than the former. If one stands back from the lesson what are the children doing? It could be argued that they are undertaking a shape recognition task. A child much younger than a Year 2 could undertake this activity because all they are doing is analysing whether "one shape is similar to another". It is pure pattern recognition, there is little understanding about the true learning of angle, which of

7

course is that angle is a measure of turn, which is measured using a unit called degrees and that when one turns 90 degrees the consequent angle is called a "right angle".

The reason for the paucity of learning in the activity is because the lesson hinges around the "curriculum objective" rather than the learning objective" To be fair the Numeracy Strategy document makes a clear distinction between the two. So whilst the document does indeed state that "pupils should know a quarter turn is a right angle" this is articulated under the heading "As outcomes Year 2 pupils should..." These objectives are outcome driven and state what the child should achieve at the end of their learning not the learning to be undertaken through the unit of work. The column "Pupils should be taught" is the area from which the true "learning objective" should be drawn. Here the document states that "pupils should be taught to understand angle as a measure of turn"

This distinction transforms the lesson completely. The focus for the lesson is now drawn from the learning, which involves children having an activity that relates more closely to them being able to explore the concept of angle as a measure of turn. The lesson should then develop activities which build on the learning rather than bypassing the learning process and leapfrogging on to an activity that focuses on the outcome.

Example 2: Measuring length in Year 3
How understanding the learning directs the whole lesson

The teacher was looking at measuring the hall to elucidate how many tables the children would be able to fit in for a Valentine's meal they were putting on for their parents. The "outcome" was simple enough, to measure the hall and its dimensions along with the length and width of the tables that would be used. The Numeracy Strategy sets the outcome out clearly stating that *"As outcomes pupils should use a suitable measuring instrument to measure... the length of the classroom" (NNS p90)* However when the teacher analysed the lesson and the actual learning that would take place she realised that the main element of learning would not be *"How to use a metre stick"* but rather the challenge for the children would focus more on the relationship between metres and centimetres. The children would need to appreciate that 240cm could be written as 2.4m. From this it became apparent that the main learning feature in the lesson was something that related more to the concept of base 10 rather than something relating to pure measurement. This had a major impact on the planning because once the core of the lesson was deemed to centre on *"Know and use the relationships between familiar units"* (to be fair this is what is stated by the NNS in the pupils should be taught section) the teaching followed this theme. The lesson started with an introduction to the principles of base 10 and the lesson, including the measuring activity, was centred on this backdrop.

Teachers need to engage with the true feature of the learning in a given lesson and avoid the shallow, superficial learning which teaching from curriculum outcomes delivers. The danger is that the outcome can be reached, and the hall and tables can be measured but the tragedy is that the learning can be bypassed completely, as the focus becomes the outcome rather than the learning. This is no more apparent than in the next example.

Example 3: Teaching Similes in Year 4
The need to deconstruct the learning in a curriculum objective

As far as I can see from my reading of the original Literacy Framework there were few actual learning objectives to follow. Despite the headings which state what children should be taught the reality is that what followed was "outcome" rather than learning based. So the *instruction "to collect suitable words and phrases in order to write poems and descriptions"* (Year 3 term 1) is a great end goal but it begs the question; How does one define suitable in this context? The process of defining suitable is the first step to create a cogent and effective learning objective for the lesson.

It was with this in mind that we set about trying to produce a learning objective for a lesson on similes. The renewed framework includes this in the Poetry Unit 1 – Creating Images and as with its predecessor the document draws out a "curriculum objective" for its focus when it says; *Children write their own poem using similes and other devices to create imagery.* Again the learning question remains; what makes a good simile? In truth this presented a challenge both to the classteacher and me as we sought to tease out the learning. What we came to appreciate was that a good simile contains a multiplicity of qualities that relate to the object for comparison rather then just a single feature. So whilst we all know that the "bright, shiny, golden penny" would be a better simile to describe the sun than the "fresh, ripe tomato" we need to be in a position to articulate to the child why one is better than the other. If we cannot do so then the lesson will fall into the trap of relying purely on osmosis and the teacher is left hoping that the child can "see" that one is better than the other and then somehow come up with one similar for themselves. This might be possible for the more able child with a breadth of language and a slice of luck in choosing the right words at the right time but this approach often leaves the less able floundering.

Using our example the reason why the penny is better than the tomato is that the penny has a range of attributes that align to the description of the sun; the shape (round), the colour (golden), its brightness (shiny). The tomato on the other hand has only one, namely that is round. This knowledge creates a clear learning objective for the lesson and empowers the children to explore the power of simile in a clear framework. They are even able to objectively assess their understanding by simply using the number of attributes each simile contains.

What makes a good Learning Objective?

It is easy to discern if the learning objective is secure because the following features will all be present:

There will be a tight bite-size focus for each lesson. Where curriculum objectives are used to drive the learning the focus for the lesson becomes very broad. As in the example above *"to use imagery in poetry"* is a curriculum not a learning objective and it is both broad and woolly. This is why oftentimes learning objectives can be found spanning a whole week's work, this is because they are outcome based and are simply objectives to be met by the child on completion of the learning not the learning itself. This process dilutes learning and leads to lessons where children meander in and around concepts, rather than the learning driven lesson which has a clear structured stepping stone approach to the learning process

Differentiation is easily discernable. Where lessons are driven by curriculum objectives, and more especially where they fall prey to the trap of osmosis, the differentiation is often by outcome rather than by learning. Whilst there are lessons where it is appropriate for the outcome to be the differentiating factor between the ability groups in the class, all too often it is a compromise brought about by the teacher's inability to perceive and tease out the true learning in a given lesson.

So the lesson based on using a range of verbs, nouns and adjectives for impact (Primary Framework) will degenerate into a subjective assessment on whether we feel the words used add impact and where they do there will be no understanding on the part of the teacher whether this has been done by chance or by design based on the learning objective. Where the learning objective clearly states that powerful adjectives are those that have limited scope in terms of their context then the children can identify the learning, assess the success of their word choice more easily and articulate why one word is better than another. Moreover because the learning has a tight focus it is easy for the teacher to add an activity to extend the more able child. The teacher might build in the challenge to use a word that is limited in context (the same as the whole class) but also is usually used in a different context. So the child who uses the word "towering giraffe" has achieved two elements of the learning. He has used a word which is more limited in scope than "tall" but also has used a derivative of the word tower which is usually used in the context of castles. This extension is only possible because the narrowing of the learning objective allows for a clear focus in the mind of both the teacher and the child. To seek to create an extension activity from the broader curriculum objective of; *use a range of verbs, nouns and adjectives for impact* would lead one to conclude that the learning would simply focus around *"use a wider range"*, which is hardly helpful or meaningful to either teacher or learner.

So too with the simile example above; whilst the bright shiny golden penny might be ideal in one context it does not sit well in the sentence; the spaceship orbited the sun which stood in the sky like a bright shiny golden penny. The subject of the sentence focuses on the orbiting spaceship, therefore the two dimensional penny now seem a little incongruous in this context. The simile needs to draw on a 3D shape to align itself with the action of the spaceship. A more staraight-forward differentiation task would be to see if the children can find words with more multiple attributes than they have already, although to be fair this is not as rich as the example above as it is simply a linear extension of the original task rather then one that creates differentiation by breadth. In both examples however, it is easy to see the extension task when the learning objective is clearly delineated.

A clear learning objective also streamlines the assessment process markedly and has the added benefit of often making it objective rather than a subjective process. How does anyone possibly mark against success criteria such as *"powerful adjectives?"* I would suggest it is virtually impossible without it degenerating into subjectivity, but selecting the best adjective between big, grey or lumbering to describe the elephant in a written narrative is fairly self evident if one uses the criterion we have articulated throughout this article. It makes peer assessment a realistic proposition. How many of us have tried to get children to assess each other's work only to hear them say at the end... "I liked it". Using highly focused learning it is possible to assess outcomes objectively. One could analyse the number of attributes one simile has over another and in that sense the work is numerically quantifiable in terms of quality. This process also allows feedback to be clearly structured enabling the child to accomplish the task with a complete understanding of the principles underlying it.

Conclusion

Despite the rather disingenuous title the truth is that the role of the learning objective cannot be underestimated in its ability to drive learning forward. Sadly as Shirley Clarke found to her cost, when the principles get delivered through the hands of those who seek to relegate the art of teaching into a series of trite formulaic steps then the result is an inevitable watering down of the complex art of teaching and this will never deliver secure and robust learning in children. However for those who have thought through the issue, and are able to dovetail the pure principles into their own pedagogical understanding then the learning objective debate has the ability to transform teaching and enhance learning immeasurably.

THE LION, THE WYCHE
AND THE LEARNING

Introduction

As Lucy makes her way through the wardrobe that first time, feeling the softness of the long fur coats gradually turn into the hard, prickly branches of the trees, her world is transformed as she steps out into the wintery land of Narnia. Whilst the gas lamp flickers, looking vaguely familiar and the snow falls as it did in her earthly world she is soon to find that so much of what she learnt in her pre-wardrobe life will not equip her to cope with fauns, beavers that talk and a witch that can seemingly create Turkish delight at will. The book is a vivid and powerful description of a parallel world in which Lucy must learn afresh many of the things that she may have taken for granted and thought she had fully imbibed in her previous life. The land of Narnia provides a seemingly good analogy for the concept of "Situational Learning" A theory I stumbled across mainly by chance, in the first instance, but which has had a major impact on the teaching and learning here at The Wyche.

I have always been struck by how children appear to struggle to transfer their learning from one context to another. We have long been told that this is the hallmark of successful learning. So the received wisdom is that effective teaching can only be truly assessed when the child demonstrates an ability to apply a taught concept correctly in a fresh context. I am a great advocate of this and would not wish to undermine this vital element of teaching. I remember teaching a Year 4 class about the prevailing winds in the UK and the resultant rain shadow that falls across the country as the weather system hits areas of high altitude. I was delighted to note that the following year when the class were set the question as to why areas of Switzerland had higher snowfall than other areas one girl declared; *"We should check the prevailing wind across the country"* There should be no doubt in any of our minds that this is learning that is rich, contextualised and evidenced by a transferability that demonstrates a clear and full understanding of the concept on the part of the child. If this is true learning then why is it that so many children struggle to get to this magical point of being able to transfer their learning across contexts.

The Darts and the Maths Conundrum

Knowing that our caretaker was a keen darts player my deputy, Jon decided to use his sporting prowess in one of his Maths lessons. The children were encouraged to play Gary at darts and then to compete with him on working out the scores required to "go out" in a game of 501.[1] The sporting element was no contest as I suspected it might be but to my relative surprise the mathematical contest was no competition either.

When it came to calculating the numbers required to win the game Gary was lightning fast. Bearing in mind that the dart board contains treble scores and doubles, he weaved seamlessly through the two and three times tables using factors and combinations of numbers fluently. Not only did he totally trounce even our more able Year 6 children (many who went on to attain level 6 in their SAT papers) but as we had some visiting governors

---

[1] The rules for 501 are as follows: Each player starts with 501 points. Each player then throws three darts in turn calculating the total and subtracting it from their previous score. The winner is the player who reduces their score to exactly zero.

that morning he left both them, and sadly, it has to be said, the Headteacher completely trailing in his wake. I was astounded by his mathematical ability and asked him how he got on with Maths in school. He informed me that he had no qualifications in the subject. But it was his second comment I found more telling; he went on to say that whilst he may not have excelled in Maths at school he was good at adding and subtracting darts scores. I was left to ponder on the statement because in my own mind I had always assumed they were the same thing but this scenario left me wondering whether there was more to it.

Situated Learning Theory (Jean Lave)

It was at this point that I came across the work of Jean Lave and the concept of "Situated Learning". In 1988 Lave worked alongside housewives in Irvine, California. She noted that when they were supermarket shopping they used complex mathematics to explore the comparative prices of products. However what she also found was that when they were given the identical calculations in a classroom environment they were unable to complete the tasks to the same level of competence. So whilst they were scoring 98% effectiveness in the supermarket this dropped to an average of 59% when tested in the classroom. Similar studies showed a comparable pattern. The market traders in Recife, Brazil generated correct answers 99% of the time when running their stalls but in a classroom situation, with a pen and paper their scores dropped to 74%. (Carraher and Schliemann, 2002) In a similar experiment workers in a dairy unit made virtually no mathematical errors when calculating loads for lorries leaving their depot but averaged only 64% when they were confronted with the same problems in a formal arithmetic test. (Scribner and Fahrmeier, 1982) Herndon (1971) also reported spectacular differences between the maths of the scorers in the local bowling alley and results they produced in a test simulating "bowling score problems".

These studies have spurred a raft of research exploring areas related to the concept of "Situated Learning". One piece of research showed that deep sea divers learning a set of words under the water were able to recall them a lot more effectively when back in the water as opposed to remembering them on land. This touches on another area related to "Locational Memory"; the principle that location can determine one's ability to recall information from the (seemingly) sub-conscious. Any of us who have had to go back downstairs to remember what it was they came upstairs for, has experienced this first hand!

Even more surreal is the concept of "State Dependent Learning". The University of Hull found that students taught whilst slightly intoxicated through drinking gin and tonics could recall the learning better when they entered back into an inebriated state. In similar vein rats that were taught to run a maze under the influence of a depressant drug often forgot the route when tested later without the drug. However when they were given the drug again, they retrieved their memory and ran the maze successfully.

However, all these pieces of research, as bizarre as many of them are, have one key element which is that situations, locations and more generically different contexts have a huge impact on learning. Lave *"spent several years of exploration of arithmetic as cognitive practice in practical settings that led to a kernel observation... (that) the same people differ in their arithmetic activities in different settings." (Cognition in Practice p3)* She went on to crystallise her thinking into the theory that has become known as "Situated Learning". In its simplest form it is the view that all learning is not simply the transmission of ideas and concepts from one individual to another in an abstract and decontextualised form. Instead it is a social process whereby knowledge is constructed within a particular social and physical environment. Consequently the learning will often remain in the context in which it is learnt and we should not therefore assume that because children (or even adults) have "learnt" something in one context that they will be readily able to apply it to another. There is a complexity about the transference of this newly acquired knowledge which needs to be appreciated. Simon, H.A. (1980) wrote that *"the empirical evidence for the transferability of knowledge and skills to a new task and situation is very mixed"* He went on to conclude that whilst learning transfer is not impossible *"certain specific kinds of instruction don't produce transfer"*

The common perception of learning is that children are taught concepts in the belief that knowledge is like a set of tools that they can draw on when faced with a new problem in a new context. Yet as early as 1931, Thorndike had stated in his work "The Psychology of Learning" that this thinking was flawed. The mind is not set in a contextual vacuum and this element makes learning transfer more complex than many imagine. As Lave states *"the common position on learning… is that children can be taught general cognitive skills (even if) these skills are dis-embedded from the routine contexts of their use"* The problem for schools is that most of our learning is done in this de-contextualised environment or as Mick Waters once described it; "the artificial world of the classroom".

Implications on Classroom Practice

There are two implications that we can draw from the research on situated learning. Firstly there is the issue of turning quality, interactive and contextually rich Maths teaching into the narrow pen and paper Maths required to attain a quality SAT score in the context of a test situation. Conversely there is the issue that travels in the opposite direction of turning some of our bog-standard Maths lessons into meaningful learning for the real-world.

(i) Turning practical Maths into test scores

One of the most frightening implications from the research relates to our own country's obsession with achievement in SAT tests. Whilst the vast majority of educationalists accept that the best Maths is context rich and is best taught in a real-life scenario it might be that such pedagogy finds itself at odds with the need to drive schools up the league tables.

When I became a head in 2000 I was quite determined that I was not going to be a leader of a SATs factory. We continued to teach Maths in a creative way. At the time I was a Leading Maths Teacher (a position that the National Numeracy Strategy bestowed on those who were then used to disseminate supposed good practice) and in fact all the KS2 staff had held this role at some point. In my mind the provision was excellent, the teaching of a high standard, the Maths was creative and focused on the need for children to acquire pure mathematical understanding. At the time it baffled me somewhat to find that our SAT scores plummeted downwards in these years. Whilst I did not understand the concept at the time it has become apparent to me that this was the process of situated learning in operation.

So pedagogically schools would be commended for developing mathematical understanding in the real-life context of a supermarket (if this were feasible with a class of 30 children). However whilst the children might function with accuracy in the high 90's in that environment the research from the Californian housewives shows that their SAT score would plummet to 59% when they return to the school classroom to undertake the same questions in a written test. So whilst an educational observer might be considering putting them in for the level 6 test when viewed in the shop, they have barely achieved level 4 in the classroom setting. So too with children taught alongside the traders in Recife market, their 99% accuracy would plummet to a level right on the border of level 4 or 5 when placed in a formal pen and paper situation. No two levels of progress there then!

What is more worrying is that if the research holds good and learning is context bound then it would appear that those schools with a narrow, dull paper-based worksheet/workbook based curriculum will benefit greatly when they come to be tested using a narrow, dull paper-based test. As Lave herself commented; *"classroom tests put the (situated learning) principle to work, they serve as a measure of individual 'out of context' success"*. So whilst pedagogically many may intrinsically feel that Maths taught in the "real world context" is the strongest form of learning we all know it would be a challenge to collect and collate assessment data in this arena. So in an educational culture that is obsessed with data and school comparison we revert to a standardised national test to assess children. As Jo Boaler comments; *"I would suggest that tests that are short, narrow and closed assess something that has very little educational value. Furthermore, they may target a form of school knowledge that is increasingly incompatible with the flexible and technological demands of the modern world." (Back to Basics or Forward to the Future, 2010)* Of course she is quite right but the accountability monster continues to ravage education devouring everything in its path and so schools find themselves constrained by the judgment measures used upon them.

As the Welsh Assembly stated in its report recommending the abolition of SAT tests; *"Much of the evidence received focused on the ways in which the current form of testing had impacted upon the curriculum. The group has considered whether the testing, in terms of the hard data it gives is of sufficient value to compensate for the evident impoverishment of pupil's learning" (Chapter 3.4)* So schools find themselves running into the arms of a narrow curriculum to fulfil the needs of the system and should they traverse into the pedagogically pure waters of real-life learning they run the risk of children failing to excel in the differing context of a test that assesses *"something that has very little educational value " (Boaler)* It is only the brave or the maverick that are prepared to swim against the tide and provide a Maths curriculum that is rich in depth, understanding and set in the reality of life itself.

I am often asked whether the creativity of our curriculum explains our (relatively) high scores at Key Stage 2 as children leave the school. In light of the above you will see I am wary of correlating the two. I don't think there is a direct and explicit relationship between the creativity of the curriculum offered and outcome in SAT test scores. Based on the research above, I certainly don't hold to the (often widely peddled notion) that a creative Maths curriculum has a direct causal impact on scores. What I might accede to is that the creative element makes children less fearful of playing with numbers, making their mental calculation strategies more robust and delivering a breadth of numerical understanding. I would also contend that the school's emphasis on the social and emotional curriculum allows children to work seamlessly with others and this has a major impact on their learning in a class based, peer to peer setting. But all these elements are tangential and do not impact directly or causally on the hard data which schools are called to chase in these times.[2]

(ii) Developing secure schemas

Just as it is difficult to traverse the gap from real-life learning to a pen and paper test, it is equally hard for children who are brought up on a more formal diet of Mathematics to apply their "learning" to real world situations. Whilst most of Lave's research focused on real-life mathematics and the failure of pupils to be able to transfer their learning in this sphere to the more formal arena of pen and paper Maths there is as much research that moves the other way. There is ample evidence that where Maths teaching focuses on algorithms and set procedures children struggle to apply this to situations that require a mathematical solution in the real world.

Mick Waters tells a wonderful story of children who were set the task of determining how much metal would be required to make a goal post. The children set about the task with great enthusiasm quickly measuring the posts but slowing slightly when they came to the crossbar. The initial

[2] I have written at greater length on this theme in my article "Does the creative curriculum raise standards?" available as a download from the school website

suggestion of how they might run a trundle wheel across it was quickly dismissed and the latter version of a child on shoulders with a ruler in hand was agreed to be the best option. Whilst there is an element of humour attached to the story the truth is that if the work had been presented on a worksheet similar to that on the right it is unlikely that it would have escaped the notice of any child that the opposite sides are of equal length. The point is that just because children have learnt something in the formal arena of school this should not lead us to assume they will seamlessly transfer that learning into the practical world of everyday life.

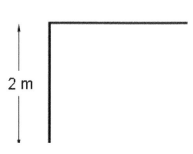

2 m

To move to the other extreme, Julie Gainsburg studied structural engineers in their working environment for over 70 hours. In that time whilst she noted that they all used Mathematics extensively, she also noted that they hardly ever resorted to any of the standard methods and procedures they would have been taught in schools. Instead they developed their own models to which they could apply mathematical methods to solve the "real-life" problems they came across. She concluded that much of the Maths taught in school with *"its focus on performing computational manipulations is unlikely to prepare students for the problem solving demands of the high tech workplace" (Gainsburg, 2003)*

In further research Lave observed that dieters who were asked to measure portions such as ¾ of two-thirds of a cup of ingredients quickly resorted to informal methods based on their "own" mathematical understanding rather applying formal algorithms they would have learnt at school. So they would measure out two-thirds of a cup and then emptying it on to a working surface would divide it into quarters and remove one of them. She noted that in the "real world" people tend to use intuitive number sense which is more consummate with their own understanding and the context in which they are working. It could be argued that they are drawing on a richer mathematical framework than that which is often delivered in formal and traditional lessons that focus solely on algorithms and procedures which allow them to pass a test at the end of their schooling.

As Jo Boaler states; *"for many years schools have been driven by the requirement to prepare students for exams at 16, exams which require the recall of facts and methods"* Even more depressing is her conclusion drawn from interviews with groups of secondary school students and quoted in her excellent book; The Elephant in the classroom. She wrote *"The student taught with traditional methods all said they used and needed Maths outside of school but that they would never make use of Maths they were learning in their classrooms. The students regarded the school mathematics classroom as a separate world with clear boundaries that separated it from their lives."*

What is the answer?

a) Real-Life Contexts

It would appear that schools are on the horns of a dilemma. If the theory of situated learning is to be believed it would appear that de-contextualised lessons will deliver what the system requires, namely good exam scores, but the children will remain impoverished in later life. However as schools seek to develop Maths in a "real-life" context then they may find their children struggle to translate this into secure test scores and this is educational suicide for schools in our present culture.

Some work by Jo Boaler might assist in this. In her article, *Making School Mathematics Real*, she tracked the mathematical progress of two schools. One had opted to put Maths into a real-life context and taught the curriculum through open-ended problems that the children were encouraged to solve. The second school introduced their children to procedures and algorithms that allowed them to work their way through a series of booklets. It has to be said that in tests carried out on both cohorts of children the overall results were not significantly different. However that is where the similarities end. What became clear from a deeper analysis of the children's workings was that the manner in which they had tackled the tasks were markedly different. The former school used intuitive and more informal methods to solve many of the problems that had been set. This would lead one to believe that there would be less of a gap between the children's *"school maths"* and the strategies they might use to solve problems in the *"real world"*. However various forms of evidence from the second cohort demonstrated clearly that *"they had developed an inert knowledge that they were rarely able to use in anything other than textbook and test situations" (Back to Basics or Forward to the Future, ATM 2010)*

In her conclusions to this research Boaler is honest enough to confess that *"there is no simple solution to the problem of transfer across contexts, or across the school-real divide"* but she goes on to say that *"I think problems will be reduced if Mathematics... acknowledges the social environment in which students are forming their understanding"*

It would appear therefore that part of the answer is to ensure that wherever possible all our Maths teaching is set in a realistic context that is relevant to the children who are working on the problem. In this scenario the Maths would become (what it should be) a tool to be used to solve a real problem. All too often Maths is presented to children as a rather abstract and irrelevant numerical code like a hidden mystery that only the teacher understands and from which the child must decipher its meaning and develop their own understanding.

So whilst we note that the Recife trader's scores dropped from nearly 100% accuracy to a score of 74% when moving from real life to classroom, I am convinced that if we reversed the process and taught them formally in a classroom (and it were possible to score their performance in the market place, which it isn't, I know) I am sure the dip in their attainment would fall well below 74%. The point I am trying to make is that those children taught in a formal context invariably have a narrow understanding of Mathematics that is non-transferable in any other scenario. Whilst the scores of the traders dipped to 74% at least they were able to take some of their Maths back into the classroom and use it effectively, albeit not to the same standard as the true life context. The teaching in context is therefore a win-win situation, except for the blight of the exam hurdle on the educational landscape.

As has been said *"The goal of school should not be to do well in school but to do well in life" (Eisner, 2004)* This being the case then many schools are failing so many children in the paucity of the Mathematical diet we are offering them. At its root the error hinges on the lack of understanding around "Situated Learning." As long as the misconception persists that all children require is a set of mathematical tools, however they are learnt or acquired and that we continue to believe that they will apply these seamlessly in a variety of contexts then we will forever be selling children short.

Guy Claxton is right when he says; *"If the core purpose of education is to give young people a useful apprenticeship in real-life learning, then the kinds of learning they do in school has to match the kinds of learning that people do in the wider world" (Guy Claxton "What's the point of school?").* If we look in the National Curriculum we find within the first few opening sentences the statement that *"schools should offer a curriculum which... prepares pupils for the opportunities, responsibilities and experiences of life."* The Maths curriculum also states in its opening paragraph that Maths is "essential to everyday life" The irony is that so much of what is taught is de-contextualised and as the situated learning research clearly shows is unlikely to benefit pupils in their "everyday life" either as children or it would appear as adults.

b) Teaching in a context rich environment

All the arguments above focus on a macro-scale of looking at the Maths Curriculum as a whole; however the "situated learning" principle can apply on a micro scale as well in terms of concept acquisition in young learners.

A few years ago we had a specialist teacher who came in to assess one of our children on the SEN register. In the course of the feedback discussion she commented on one child's ability to see a letter shape when it was written in pen but when the same letter was drawn in pencil they found it harder to distinguish. Whilst the concept of situated learning was not known to me then and the preceding discussion made no reference to it, the specialist made it clear that a change of context however minimal can cause a gulf in the child's ability to transfer learning.

What we need to appreciate therefore is that context can play a major part in learning on a micro scale. I was recently working in the Year 1 class alongside the classteacher who was delivering a great lesson on place value leading on to the children successfully adding tens onto a two digit number. Their articulation throughout the lesson and in the activities along with their accuracy in the assessment task seemed to suggest that they seemed secure in their understanding. The next day the teacher presented the children with the 100-square and asked the same questions. It was as if the new context had created a collective memory wipe in the minds of the children. When asked the simple question *"What is 34+10?"* a question they had answered effortlessly the day before, they seemingly struggled to grasp any element of the concept.

It is clear to me that for children to develop secure schemata in Mathematical constructs they need to be exposed to a wide variety of contexts, seeing and exploring concepts by virtue of a 360-degree approach. Not only does this close all doors to a "single-contextual learning" which we have seen can be flawed in developing a richness of understanding but it also allows thinking to be challenged across the spectrum thereby enriching understanding. The power of contextuality should not be lost on teachers and in fact varying contexts can be used to enhance learning rather than diminishing it.

Concluding Thoughts

The other day I came across an acquaintance from my tennis club. We were both at an opening of an art exhibition of a mutual friend, we both had that experience of catching each other's eye and to both of us it became apparent that whilst we both recognised each other neither of us were quite sure of how we knew each other, or even the name of the other person. How could this be, seeing as when we meet on a tennis court with racquet in hand we generally greet each other using our first names. Context is everything.

All this brings us full circle to our Narnia analogy. We need to appreciate that if education was just a simple case of filling the mind with a set of de-contextualised facts, procedures and principles then teachers wouldn't need training and a computer would be as good a resource to learn from as any human being. However if we understand the nuances and the complexities of learning and that context is everything then we will come to appreciate that the short trip through the wardrobe puts every child into a new land and therefore a new context which will challenge their true understanding of learnt concepts. If we are to educate children for life rather than simply for exams then children will need to be immersed in a Maths curriculum that is open ended and set in contexts that are as close to real life learning as the teachers can manage in the "artificial world we call the classroom" (Mick Waters)

WHY DID I HAVE TO BE
BORN IN AUGUST?
THE SUMMER BORN DEBATE

Preface

It was some time ago now that I was a class teacher in a school where the register was in birth order from September to August. I couldn't help noticing a slender correlation between the birth dates of the children and their seeming academic standing in the class. In those days I simply logged the pattern with a mild form of interest and focused back on the teaching. However in recent years the drive to raise standards for every group of children within a given school means that data has poured into schools at a frightening rate and the issue of the "Summer Born" children has become a major aspect of the debate.

The "Summer-Born" Achievement Gap

The correlation I spotted anecdotally all those years ago has become an incontestable piece of statistical data and the issue of raising standards amongst "Summer Born" children has become high stakes within the system. Raise Online now includes data for children born in each of the three terms in the academic year allowing schools to determine if the summer-born are making less progress than their peers. The issue was brought to a head recently with the publication of a document from the Institute for Fiscal Studies entitled *"When you are born matters: evidence for England"* They determined that those born in in the latter stages of the academic year are 5.4% more likely to be on the SEN register at age 11, 6.4% less likely to achieve 5 GCSE at grades A-C, 2% less likely to go to university and 1% less likely to graduate with a degree. Indeed some of their graphs show a frightening correlation:

Figure 3.1. Proportion of pupils obtaining at least the expected level at Key Stages 1, 2, 3 and 4 (ages 7, 11, 14 and 16), by date of birth

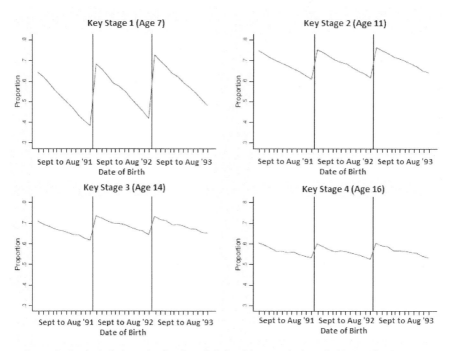

Source: Authors' calculations using Key Stage 1, 2, 3 and 4 test results from the National Pupil Database for pupils born in 1990–91, 1991–92 and 1992–93.

The report hit the headlines not for its data which is generally well attested to in educational circles but for their rather radical proposal that there should be a weighting principle when calculating exam related scores. They recommend that all national achievement scores should be "age adjusted" to ensure that *"those born towards the end of the academic year are not disadvantaged by taking the tests younger"* It is an interesting solution to the problem and has promoted a lot of debate but I fear there may be another more simple resolution that actually hits at the heart of all teaching and learning in schools and will therefore benefit all children whatever their age or ability.

Whilst the evidence is clear that the summer born appear to struggle to achieve, the truth is that the gap narrows as children get older. The graphs appear to show an alarming correlation between age and achievement and allude to the fact that there is a debate to be had but they also demonstrate the closing of the gap over time. The statistics presented above show a diminishing number of percentage points difference as children get older. This is not to conclude that there is not an issue to be addressed it is simply to state the obvious fact that when a child born in August lands in a reception class at the age of 4 with a child who is just on the cusp of their 5th birthday, the age gap is more marked. A whole year separates them but more importantly the older child has been on the planet 20% longer than his younger classmate. By the time both children leave university at the age of 22 the older child has only spent 4.6% longer, thus producing a tailing off effect as age increases. The report itself acknowledged that the trend does not continue into adulthood. The Institute for Fiscal Studies wanted to use this time lag as a statistical basis for adjusting scores but as intimated earlier, learning is too complex to reduce down to bald statistics. However I always take a somewhat more simplistic stance and believe that the best place to find answers to issues of Teaching and Learning is in pedagogy not in statistical or data adjustment (although this might have a place in some instances)

Resolving the "Summer-Born" Achievement Gap

It would be hard to argue against the simplistic argument of "time spent on the planet" as being a contributing factor and in truth few would deny that this is a contributing cause. But are there other reasons which would allow us to be more pro-active in our response rather than simply rolling over and giving into the fact that a date of birth condemns a child to a life of underachievement?

The Outliers

A starting point might be to look at Malcolm Gladwell's startling finding in his book "The Outliers". Whilst at a "hockey game" (an ice hockey match, to those this side of the Atlantic) Gladwell noticed an interesting pattern in the birthdates of the players. The majority of them were born in the early months of the year. Indeed upon further investigation this trend continued with a seemingly strong correlation between the months of the year and the number of players in the NHL. Realising that this was either an example of unparalleled co-incidence or a definable pattern he looked into other sports. He noted the players in the Premier League in England had a similar pattern except that their "Golden" month was September and the numbers then declined throughout the year to August.

Month	Players
January	51
February	46
March	62
April	49
May	46
June	49
July	36
August	41
September	36
October	34
November	33
December	30

This second correlation provided Gladwell with the insight he needed to propose an underlying reason for the trend. In the US and Canada, the cut off for eligibility for the junior hockey leagues is January 1st. The implication of this is that when the teams are chosen, those born in

September have one unique and obvious advantage over those born later on in the year – they are older! In the case of the under 8 team, the child born on January 1st is not only almost a whole year older than a child born on 31st December but he has also lived nearly 12% longer. He will in general terms be stronger, taller and possibly more co-ordinated than his August born peer. The same principle transfers itself seamlessly into the Premier League in England where the cut-off date for eligibility is September 1st. No surprise to find therefore that the upper echelons of football in the UK are dominated by players born in the autumn.

So how does it work? The coaches of the local teams assess the ability of the children that come to the open training sessions. From there they select those demonstrating the most potential and those that exhibit the early signs of a budding talent. As Gladwell notes most of these will, by definition, be the older children simply due to the fact that their age provides them with a greater opportunity to shine. They are then put in the team and start to play competitive matches. At times they are drawn away from the main squad for elite training and so the gap between the two groups widens and those spotted early are given additional opportunities to foster their natural talent.

Academics have called this principle the "relative-age effect" thereby acknowledging that this initial gain attributable to age gets turned into a more profound advantage over time. It is similar to the infamous "Matthew effect", based on the verse from the New Testament, *"For whoever has will be given more, and they will have an abundance. Whoever does not have, even what they have will be taken from them."* (Matthew 25:29) The principle underlying this is that those who are deemed to have a natural talent progress at a greater rate simply by virtue of the fact that additional opportunities are opened up to them.

The tragedy of the "relative-age effect" is that the differentiation of both perceived ability and therefore provision for the groups of children is based on something as spurious as their date of birth. It is not difficult to see how this applies directly to the "Summer Born" debate. Those who come to school born in September are nearing their fifth birthday; some of those who are taught alongside them will have just turned four in the previous month. The teacher receives the children and, rightly to a certain extent, notes that some of the children appear somewhat more advanced in certain areas of the curriculum and therefore wishes to differentiate for their needs. It doesn't take a huge leap of imagination to work out that many of these will be the September born as they have spent nearly 20% more time living and learning than some of their peers. The groups are therefore distilled throughout the academic year and those children deemed more able are given a level of academic provision that only reinforces the divide between them and their peers.

If the "relative-age effect" was the only principle at work in the classroom all might be relatively fine and easy to adjust, however the situation is compounded by the "Pygmalion effect" an older and yet still highly significant piece of research from the 1960's.

The Pygmalion Effect

In 1965 Robert Rosenthal and Lenore Jacobson undertook a seminal study looking at the role of teacher expectation on the attainment of children. Both men had spent years in education and both had become convinced that a teacher's low expectation of children, especially those in socio-economically deprived areas, were contributing to the high failure rate amongst students. They therefore undertook a simple experiment. Working in a predominantly lower-class area in a challenging school they informed the teachers that they were running a test on the children that they entitled "The Harvard Test of Inflected Acquisition." They told the school that the test would not only determine the child's IQ but would also be able to identify those children who were in a position to make rapid and above average progress. At the start of the year the teachers were given the names of the children that the test had concluded would make additional progress. In reality the test measured no such thing and the names of the children were simply a sample taken at random by the two researchers.

However at the end of the year the children were retested on their IQ. Those in the "rapid progress" groups made 50% more progress than those in the "normal" groups showing an average rise of 12 points compared with the 8 points progress of their peers. The results were more pronounced in the younger children where the infant children showed an increase of over 20 points or more. Equally as interesting were the subjective elements of the research. The teacher assessments, such as the reading grades, followed a similar pattern. The teachers also shared that they found the "special" students were better behaved, more engaged in the learning and were generally more amenable and friendly than their counterparts

Rosenthal and Jacobson concluded that a self-fulfilling prophecy had occurred and that the expectations of the teachers had subtly and sub-consciously impacted greatly on the learning and attainment of the students. In short the expectation had become the main driver and the key factor in determining the progress made by each child.

There is a dramatic anecdotal story that has been told in educational circles for many years. It may fall into the category of an urban myth but Christina Hoff Sommers, quotes it in her book "The War Against Boys" and claims in her end notes that it is a story told by Dr Carl Boyd. The story runs that a well-respected teacher, Mrs Daughty, taught in one of the Chicago schools. One year she found her sixth grade class difficult to handle and drew the conclusion that many of them must have special educational needs. One evening she was working late at the school and went into the school office to look at the files where the IQ scores were held. To her astonishment she found that the majority of the students in her class had above average intelligence, many having IQ scores in the 120's and 130's with one child having an IQ of 145. She concluded from this that the issue with the class was that the work they had undertaken lacked challenge and their poor behaviour was a direct consequence of this. She therefore determined to raise the challenge of the work and set higher expectations throughout the class as a whole. By the end of the year the children had outperformed any previous year group and became noted in the school for their good behaviour. The principal was keen to know the secret of the teacher's success and she confided in him that she had taken a sneak preview of their IQ scores earlier in the year. He felt under obligation to inform her that the numbers were not their IQ scores but their locker numbers!

Whether the story is true or not we may never be sure but either way it demonstrates, in narrative form, the reality of the "Pygmalion Effect" and the fact that a teacher's expectation of a class or even of an individual child has a huge impact on their social, emotional and academic progress.

Am I doomed because I was born in August?
(Answers from a non-educational source)

Therefore, we have two factors intertwined that work against the summer born child both powerful in their own right but both redeemable in educational terms. The problem for both is that there is an underlying principle of low expectation built in which is compounded when there is no freedom for children to move forward in a clear framework of progression.

So the August born child may never enter the first team because the expectations of the coach are set too low and the system is too rigid to allow free-flow as players improve. Therefore the better players continue with the superior provision and the Matthew Effect kicks in as a natural consequence. Away from education there has been a raft of research which has shed new light on this issue and seeks to propose solution that run counter to the seemingly natural process of inertia that can exist in this area. The most academically robust in terms of quantitative and qualitative research is Carol Dweck's work on "Mindsets", but books such as "Bounce" by Matthew Syed and "Talent is Overrated" by Geoff Colvin underscore the central theme of Dweck's work.

I have written about Carol Dweck's work elsewhere so a brief summary will suffice here, but she challenges the traditional notion of self-esteem, that children will suffer emotional damage if they are seen to fail. The perceived wisdom of many is that we should bolster children at every point, always looking for the positive in everything and reducing the possibility of any negative outcomes. The tragedy is that this builds in children, what Dweck calls, a "Performance Orientation" where the performance is everything and becomes the only thing that matters. The reality is that many of the children on this continuum, often more able teenage girls, crash and burn when they discover that not everything comes easily to them or they hit a specific cul-de-sac in an area of learning. They draw the conclusion that "they are not bright" and emotionally this has a dramatic impact on their ability to engage in future learning. Dweck says that we should be taking children on a very different trajectory. Her research shows that those who become sustained learners and move on to maximise their potential are those who have a "Learning Orientation". These children have been taught that learning is a process rather than an end goal. It reflects Guy Claxton's comment that *"you only learn when you are in the fog"* So whilst the performance orientated child would see this as "failure" and would draw negative conclusions about their ability based on their performance, the learning orientated child sees this apparent stumbling block as a natural part of the learning process and concludes that good progress is being made. You won't need me to tell you that our national education system is riddled with "Performance Orientation" as schools seek to make children hit certain levels at certain ages to clamber up the league table. It is not surprising therefore to find that many of our children are weighed down by the need to perform and consequently their learning, and more especially their attitude to learning, suffers accordingly.

Matthew Syed's book "Bounce" draws on similar concepts but from a different angle. There is a generally accepted notion, that sportsman such as Matthew (England table tennis number one for almost a decade) rise to such heights through something we often label as "natural talent". Matthew challenges this view contending that far from just pure talent it is practice and tenacity that allows people to succeed in any given field of expertise. His thesis, developed out of one simple observation: If talent is the key factor in determining sporting success how was it that the street in which Matthew was brought up managed to spawn twelve table tennis stars within his generation? To seek to explain this in terms of statistical correlation of chance would somehow beggar belief. In which case how could it be that if talent is the only reason for success that so many table tennis champions lived in Silverdale Road in the town of Reading? As Matthew explains the real reason did not lie in "talent" alone (although this may certainly have been one of the contributing factors) but was probably more due to the presence of one man; Peter Charters. He explains in his book... *Mr Charters was a teacher at the local primary school, a tall man with a moustache, a twinkle in his eye and a disdain for conventional teaching methods. But Charters cared about one thing above all: table tennis. He was the nation's top coach and a senior figure in the English Table Tennis Association. No child who passed through Aldryngton School in Reading was not given a try-out by Charters - and such were his zeal, energy and dedication to table tennis that anybody who showed potential was persuaded to take his or her skills forward at the local club. And so it was that a table tennis dynasty was born.*

However there is more to the story that just an inspirational teacher. Whilst Peter Charters may have been the catalyst, the real reason for the succession of table tennis stars lay elsewhere. Dr K Anders Ericsson studied violinists at the Music Academy in West Berlin as part of his research into "Expert Performance". The musicians fell into three clear groups, those who went on to become solo concert performers, those who did not attain to this but played in some of theworld's top orchestras and those who, whilst talented, were unable to aspire to either of these and reverted to becoming teachers of the instrument: Three groups and three levels of attainment, in their chosen profession. Ericsson started to trawl through data to see whether there was any correlation between those who achieved so much and those who comparatively were unable to reach such heights. They studied socio-economic background, the age they started to learn the instrument and many other factors but in the final analysis the only one which stood up to any statistical correlation was the amount of hours practiced. The elite group had put in 10,000 hours of practice, the orchestral players, 8,000 and the teachers 6,000. The rule was never broken, all 10,000-hour students were in the top category and no 6,000 hour student appeared in either of the upper two tiers. They concluded, *"The differences between expert performers and normal adults reflect a life-long persistence of deliberate effort to improve performance"* This work has led to "The 10,000 rule" which is used to offer an explanation for the disparities in seeming ability between groups in all fields of expertise.

Malcolm Galdwell cites the research in his book "Outliers" saying *"The striking thing about Ericsson's study is that he and his colleagues couldn't find any "naturals", musicians who floated effortlessly to the top while practicing a fraction of the time their peers did. Nor could they find any "grinds", people who worked harder than everyone else, yet just didn't have what it takes to break the top ranks."*

Whilst acknowledging the huge influence that Peter Charters had on his table tennis career Matthew Syed is convinced that it was the hours he undertook in sustained practice that was to be the major factor in his later success as an adult. (Olympian Matthew Syed's story - BBC website) He spent hours playing the game on the table in the garage, further time in the after school club, but more important than these was the access he had to the local table tennis club. The clubhouse was "essentially a wooden shack" (his own words) but significantly it was open 24 hours a day, just for table tennis. All the young people had a set of keys and the hours they clocked up in those days allowed them to easily fulfil the 10,000 hour rule with consummate ease. He has little doubt that this was the one determining factor that drove his success as a professional sportsman.

There are many who would argue anecdotally that the 10,000 hour rule has been validated in many sports. It is said that Andre Agassi hit a million balls a year in his pursuit of excellence. Tiger Woods stared playing golf when he was two years old and Serena Williams at the age of 3. Even those cited by many as prodigies, such as Mozart for example, are found to unearth a different story when their lives are delved into. Mozart had put in 3,500 hours by the time he was 6 and continued to study for a further 18 years before he wrote his piano concerto No 9 at the age of 21.

Geoff Colvin develops these ideas further in his book "Talent is Overrated" and introduces the principle of "deliberate practice" This is practice that is designed to improve performance. His thesis is that not all practice delivers exceptional performance. For instance, 10,000 hours of practicing a poor golf swing will deliver an even poorer golf swing! However where practice is "deliberate" and targeted then the 10,000 hours principle will start to kick in.

It is interesting to note that Matthew Syed points out that when he showed his parents the draft of his book they "disputed its entire thesis" They continue to declare that Matthew's success was "an inspirational triumph against the odds" but we live in a culture that is driven by a deep sense of meritocracy and hence we intrinsically value the notion that people are "gifted" or "talented" rather than the fact that they simply worked harder to get where they are than anyone else.

Am I doomed because I was born in August?
(Answers from an educational source)

The views espoused in the paragraphs above dovetail seamlessly into the teaching and learning debate. The education system is one that is sadly rooted in a "performance culture" and has a long standing tradition of believing that intelligence and any resulting attainment is down to birth and a quirk of genetics that remain fixed through a person's lifetime.

This was the view that Binet held when he invented the IQ test in the early part of the 20th Century. His contention was that intelligence was fixed and therefore the test would elucidate those children for whom remedial help was required. The 11+ exam was based on the same principle, namely that if intelligence is fixed then it should be possible to design a test that affirms the innate level of intelligence in a child and this can then be used as the basis for assigning them to either a Grammar or a Secondary Modern School. To be fair there are many in education who have moved away from this model already but the research stated above runs completely counter to these views and sees intelligence as a more elastic and flexible concept.

These principles don't just rest in debates around the wider education system they operate at a micro level within schools and within classrooms. Jo Boaler in her excellent book "The elephant in the classroom" points out that 88% of children put in lower ability groups early in their educational careers remain there until they leave school. Whilst every class should have elements of differentiation woven into the teaching and learning and may even group children to facilitate this, there is research that would appear to demonstrate that formal setting does leave children entrenched in the same group for a disproportionate amount of time. Even if they were to have a light bulb moment in a particular lesson they often have nowhere to go because the teaching is established at a single level from the outset, and if it isn't, then why set anyway?

Herein then lies the solution for the summer born child. Their future success depends on a cultural shift away from a "fixed mindset" (Dweck's language) where intelligence is set and outcomes are therefore essentially predetermined at birth, towards a "growth mindset" where everyone is deemed to have potential and learning is seen in the context of an ever expanding continuum not a goal to be attained.

There are two key areas upon which this hinges. Firstly there needs to be a shift in the expectations of teachers so that any glass ceiling for any child (not just the summer born) is removed. Then secondly, to facilitate this teachers need to develop a form of classroom management within their teaching that allows a fluidity of differentiated learning to occur.

Relating to the first point is the work of Hay McBer. They were commissioned by the government to look at why some teachers were more effective than others. Their conclusions were numerous, as one might expect, but a key factor both in primary and secondary schools was the teacher's ability to set "High Expectations". They wrote; *"Effective teachers set high expectations for the pupils and communicate them directly to the pupils. They challenge and inspire pupils, expecting the most from them, so as to deepen their knowledge and understanding. The most effective teachers determine the appropriateness of objectives for pupils by some form of differentiation. At its lowest level, this means expecting different outcomes from pupils of varying ability. At a more sophisticated level teachers know and use an extensive repertoire of means of differentiation – so that they are able to cope with the needs of more and less able pupils. But within these parameters effective teachers are relentless in their pursuit of a standard of excellence to be achieved by all pupils, and in holding fast to this ambition. These expectations are high, clear and consistent.*

It is the phrase... *"effective teachers are relentless in their pursuit of a standard of excellence to be achieved by all pupils"* that holds the key. If

41

our teaching is truly child centric then it should start with the child wherever they are and what ever month they happened to be born in. So whilst the younger child may find work differentiated on a lower level as they enter school, the true constructivist teacher will ensure that high expectations are set for them, rather than allowances being made for their age, this in turn will maximise progress.

However it is the second aspect that holds the greater potential for change. Schools need to develop learning structures where any setting or grouping is not so rigid that it prevents children from moving seamlessly between ability groups. At The Wyche we have developed a fluid form of differentiation in lessons such as Maths. Whilst the teacher may teach a core concept to the whole class (e.g. subtraction) and the children may well be nominally grouped according to ability in terms of the seating plan, the children will then have the freedom to decide where they want to pitch in when undertaking consolidation work. Thus the teacher will present a series of sums on the board ranging from basic TU-TU through to subtracting decimals and the children will select those they feel offer them the correct amount of challenge or as Vygotsky might put it, allows them to learn with the "zone of proximal development". Children are thus able to move fluidly through their learning sometimes deciding to drop back and consolidate a little when they have overstretched themselves or challenging themselves further once they have grasped a concept at a given level.

This is a feature of Wroxham School which was one of the schools in the *"Learning Without Limits"* project undertaken by Cambridge University. At Wroxham the children *"are not placed in ability groups but are trusted to make wise choices about how much challenge they are ready for within a range of tasks. This pedagogy has enabled a culture of intrinsic motivation and challenge to develop"* (Leadership Focus p47 Sept 2013)

This approach offers a more malleable, and therefore by definition, a more powerful form of differentiation. Of course it hinges on how deeply the "growth mindset" has been embedded into the ethos of the school and into the psyche of each child. But with this in place it not only has the potential to accelerate progress academically but also provides the student with the opportunity to become a more independent learner as they take responsibility for their own learning journey.

This style of open-ended teaching has huge implications for the "summer born" debate because if we can place children in this arena then it is conceivable that we can rethink our approach to teaching without preconceptions of a child's ability at all. It allows those in the lower echelons of the "Birth Date" calendar to push themselves as far as they can offering them the possibility to ape their older peers should they wish or be able. It is approaches such as these that can break the stranglehold that some classroom structures impose on children and free them to move unfettered through the full attainment spectrum in any given lesson; thereby removing the glass ceiling that setting, grouping and teacher preconception can impose on children and their learning and releasing teachers from feeling that they and the children they teach are held to ransom simply on the basis of the month in which they were born.

CONFUSION ENHANCES LEARNING.
DISCUSS.

Preface

A few weeks ago a friend and colleague from another school asked if they could observe one of my Maths lessons. As I still teach this is not an uncommon request and of course the flattery and the massaging of the ego that attend it are most welcome. So it was that we ended up in our Year 3 class teaching the children the finer points of fractions. Drawing the fraction ½ on the board we embarked on a discussion about what the two numbers stood for. I was initially content with the answer that; *the two was how many bits you split it into whilst the top number stood for how many pizzas you had altogether* always aware that reasoning and dialogue lie at the heart of all good Maths teaching and that quality discussion is able to tease out such misconceptions.

However within a few minutes the lesson had started to nose dive, in hindsight I probably allowed the misconception to remain for too long and this led the children into a morass of confused thinking. Over the next few minutes I realised to my horror that the lesson was in complete free fall, misconceptions were articulated with seemingly great authority by the children and I sensed that the misperceptions picked up earlier in the lesson were becoming further ingrained in the children's thinking. It was at this point in the lesson that I heard one of the year four girls announce to her friend in a voice audible enough for myself and my (no doubt bewildered) colleague to hear; *"I'm really confused"*

With my reputation as a Maths teacher of any standing in complete tatters, and only ten minutes of the lesson left I discussed with the classteacher (an NQT, just to add insult to injury) whether we could fold the lesson and whether she would graciously do something else with the class before they went to lunch. Her reply surprised me, as she claimed that the children were actually developing a measure of understanding and encouraged me to continue. We pressed on throwing further fractions at children, and amazingly the children did seem to be appearing up from the mire that was my lesson and gaining a grasp of some of the concepts. Towards the end of the lesson we asked them to discuss whether 4/4 was a fraction; to my surprise they were not daunted by this or by the concept of 6/4 which most readily drew in symbols as six quarters.

My own confusion was only accentuated by dropping into my Year 5 class and posing them the same question. Only half the children believed that 6/4 was a true fraction, the rest were either confused by the seeming numerical discrepancy or claimed that you could not have a numerator larger than a denominator. Initially I was encouraged that half had obviously grasped the notion of improper fractions, but even this bubble was burst when most of the children disclosed that they believed it was a fraction because although they were totally confused by the numbers it looked like a fraction because it had a line in the middle. My misery was made complete when a new child to the school informed me that whilst he did not understand it, he knew it was a fraction because his last teacher had told him it was. Only three children had any notion that the fraction related to a number larger than a whole. As the year 5 teacher is one of the school's most competent mathematicians on the staff it might appear to the untrained eye that the issue relates to the teaching, in the sense that the poorer it is the more progress the children make and the more qualified the teacher and the more excellent the teaching the more the children are seemingly thwarted in their learning. With these counter intuitive thoughts buzzing in my head I decided to delve into this further.

Reflecting on the Lesson further

Not only is it counter intuitive to believe poor teaching aids learning it also goes against all known research so what factor was it that led the children to make so much progress in a lesson that many would have deemed to have been so poor?

What struck me in the early part of my reflections was the simple fact that where the teacher is not driving the learning then the children themselves need to be taking up the slack. I do believe this goes some way to answering the question but that still leaves us with the conclusion that poorer teaching leads to stronger learning and this cannot be the case.

I then started to reflect on how we teach Mathematics and the role of the teacher within it. Our default method of teaching is that we take a concept and then seek to explore this with children in the most linear and simple way possible so that the children don't get confused. So, staying with the concept of fractions, I might decide to teach the simple concept of fractions using the following diagrams:

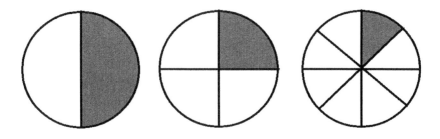

The reasoning is that fractions are a hard concept to comprehend so the simpler we make it for children the better it will be for them. Therefore the only variable that has changed has been the denominator. The shape is the same, the colour is the same, and even the position of the shaded numerator is the same (i.e. in the top right of the shape) everything is in place for the child to fully understand the principle without the clutter of having to take on any other distracting factors. We have made the path of learning uncluttered and straightforward for them, which surely is what teachers ought to do.

I have shown the following diagram (right) to various groups of teachers always posing the same question: *What fraction is being shown?* Interestingly the answer is always the same; ¾ (although some question whether the fraction is the missing ¼ or the ¾ that are shaded). However, neither of these answers is correct. When one looks more closely at the shape we realise that of course the fraction is 3/3. So how come so many of

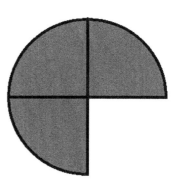

us make the mistake of thinking that the shape has anything to do with quarters? I was once posed the question whilst on a Mathematics course; *Is it possible to teach fractions without using the word - Pizza"* The comment was tongue in cheek but demonstrated the problem with so much of our Maths teaching. In our desire to make the complex accessible for children we seek to oversimplify the teaching and this often leaves children with a very narrow and shallow understanding of a given concept. The reason that so many of us see the diagram above as quarters is because our minds have developed a schema that readily accepts that the concept of the "whole" as being the whole circle (or pizza!). Your brain therefore sub-consciously fills in the missing circumference thus compounding and cementing the error of your thinking.

I suspect there is likely to be less confusion when working out the fraction involved in the two shapes to the right. This is because the schema is broken and the 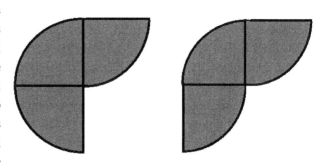 presentation of these shapes in a format that is not well established enables you to see clearly that the shape is divided into three clear sections and therefore assists you in your ability to calculate the fraction accurately.

This led me to think that whilst all concepts need to be scaffolded for children and structured in a manner that makes grasping the concept possible, it should not be done in a manner that constricts the option for children to undertake some deep learning on the way. I have come to see that much of our teaching of Maths has the potential to become so narrow and structured that it drives erroneous beliefs deeper. It is not that we are teaching direct error such as when some teachers tell children that to multiply by 10 they should just "add a zero" This is plainly false as anyone who has sought to multiply 1.8 x 10 will readily evidence. However sometimes we teach in a manner that is so narrow that it allows misconceptions to take root alongside the true mathematical concepts we are seeking to instil. I am minded of the oft quoted *"All that is necessary for evil to triumph is for good men to do nothing"*; so in this case all that is necessary for misconception to prevail is for the teacher to be negligent in presenting a concept in its fullest form.

For instance I wonder if the fractions we saw earlier would be better taught in the following conceptual framework;

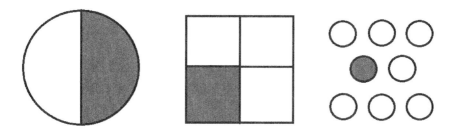

But surely this will be more confusing for children? Initially this may well be the case but it will shift the focus in the lesson away from the teacher driving the agenda that all too often leads along a narrow path of restricted learning, often driven, in many classes, by the end goal of correct worksheet completion. Instead children will be forced to look afresh at the concepts they thought they understood and which they are now being asked to apply in a fresh context. It is this element of apparent "confusion" that would appear to enhance the learning. It drives a deeper engagement from the learner and delivers a richer understanding of the underlying mathematical concepts being explored.

Dylan Wiliam illustrated this wonderfully when he asked teachers at a recent conference to draw an upside down triangle. As you can imagine the majority of those present drew something similar to the shape on the left. Yet when we stop and think about it there can be no "upside down" triangle in the truest mathematical sense of the word, a triangle is simply a shape with three angles and therefore three sides whichever way up it is. Why are we happy to draw the triangle "upside down?" It is simply because our schema for the properties of the shape have been driven by narrow teaching that has allowed us to develop the idea that any "proper" triangle should be presented with the widest horizontal line on its base.

This is further compounded when one comes to work out the area of the triangle because we have all been told that the formula is ½ base x height. But on our "upside down" triangle where is the base? Or are we assuming that there is no time in their life when children will need to work out the area of a triangle that is not set on its "base?" It might make

working out the area of this building a little interesting, as well as dangerous if you are the engineer or the quantity surveyor using the base to measure the area!

It is why the following question in one of the recent SAT papers becomes a challenge for many children because "everyone knows" that a square is the

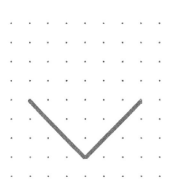

shape you can put a door and four windows in and if you just add a triangular roof you will have a perfectly formed house. This single faceted approach leads children to develop a very narrow schema for the concept of a square, therefore when asked to; *Draw two lines to complete the square?* They fail to see that the shape can be successfully completed by drawing a "square at 45°" (as many children might articulate it). Indeed children lower down in the school have often told me that the completed shape is not a square – again confirming their narrow schema view. Instead they proudly declare that the shape is in fact a "diamond", it would have been better if they had said it was a "kite" as at least that is a shape with some mathematical content to it, but a diamond is simply a *"precious mineral formed from a metastable allotrope of carbon"* and has nothing to do with mathematics whatsoever!

Can confusion aid the Learning Process?

When children (and adults for that matter) engage in a piece of learning they come to the table with underpinning preconceptions related to the task in hand. For progress to be made the children need to go through a process that social psychologists term "Cognitive Dissonance". Our experience of life causes us to construct a cognitive framework that enables us to make sense of the world. These constructs become our norm and form a set of core beliefs about the way we perceive the world. We don't stop to question whether the sun will rise in the morning or whether apples fall downwards when we drop them because we all know these things to be true. In the majority of cases these paradigms serve us well and release our mind to focus on higher order thinking, however if they are narrow in substance then all future learning that seeks to build on them will be flawed. The upside down triangle is a case in point. When a child is first presented with such a drawing their original construct of what a triangle is comes under challenge. There are elements of the shape which might confirm it as a triangle but if we have always come to believe that triangles have "a base" then we find our view challenged by this new representation of a shape we thought we understood. This is the process of "Cognitive Dissonance". The mind is challenged and confused by the new perception and must engage afresh with a concept it thought it understood.

As Guy Claxton says; *"If you are not in a fog you are not learning"* and the fog he is referring to is simply a metaphor for the process of cognitive dissonance. As the brain always seeks a harmonious and consistent belief system there is therefore a deep motivational drive to reduce dissonance within the mind. This provides a strong motivation for children to engage with the learning and to enter the process of either altering existing cognitions, add new ones to create consistency or reduce the importance of one of the dissonant elements.

Challenging current widely held perceptions and provoking children to consider areas in which they traditionally feel secure is therefore the pre-cursor to quality learning. For instance, if you fold your arms then you will observe that this has become an almost automatic, sub-conscious response. Now try to fold them the other way; what did you notice? If you did it without putting the book down first you probably noticed that you now have to pick it up off the floor (!) but you more than likely noticed that you had to think about what you were doing. The principle holds that deeper learning is taking place because confusion is setting in and the brain has to engage with the fact you are asking your arms to do the exact opposite of what, for your body, has become the norm over time.

As an aside this is why many teachers have found the use of statements more effective in provoking a depth of discussion than the asking of questions. The former allows the mind to be challenged by a statement that the listener may not be able to fit into their current construct. The danger of questions is that they can be answered easily simply by drawing on the child's current thinking whether this is in fact right or wrong. There is probably going to be more mileage and depth of discussion delivered from the statement *"some squares have five sides"* rather than the question *"how many sides does a square have?"*

The research of Derek Muller is interesting in this regard. He explored the learning of students who were being taught through online science videos. The short 10 minute clips were created by the Khan Academy and were designed to present complex scientific information in a meaningful and instructive manner for students. Muller noticed an interesting phenomenon occurring when students engaged with the video in terms of their learning.

He began by getting students to answer an initial question on an aspect of the Science curriculum; they then watched a video relating to the subject in question. The students were then asked to describe the impact of the video presentation. They all commented that the presentation was "clear", "concise" and "easy to understand". They also felt that the videos increased their confidence in being able to answer the question. However, the most interesting aspect of this part of the research was that the scores drawn from the test after the video showed little improvement when compared with their previous scores. The pre-test scores of 6.0 increased marginally to a new average score of 6.3.

Muller noted that whilst the students all described the videos as helpful with a consequent increase in their confidence their actual attainment showed little change. In his quest for answers he interviewed all the students and found some interesting patterns. Many of them could not recall accurately the information that they had seen on the video only a few minutes earlier. However, more significantly another student stated; *it wasn't that hard to pay attention because I already knew what she was talking about. So I was listening but I wasn't really paying my utmost attention"* The reality started to unfold that the students did not listen because they felt that what they were being taught already fitted into a well-structured schema they had previously developed in their studies. These deeply held beliefs and constructs would appear to thwart the mind's ability to take on board new concepts that challenged preconceived notions. In short the lack of cognitive dissonance in the learning meant that the students continued to hold to (or even worse, actually build on) their misconceptions thereby preventing them from making any real academic progress.

Muller then designed a series of his own videos but the teaching had a uniquely different emphasis. They did not seek to instruct the students in a clear presentation of fact, but instead they taught using a common misconception as a starting point. For instance one of the videos showed two men discussing how long it took the earth to go around the sun, the answer given was one day; another showed a detailed, yet completely false, explanation of the forces acting on a ball being thrown into the air. As before, the students undertook a pre-test and after watching the videos Muller asked them for their thoughts. No student this time described the videos as "clear" or "easy to understand" instead the most common word used to describe them was "confusing". However the post-test score nearly doubled from 6.0 to 11.0 (c.f. the 6.3 of the previous "clear and concise" video)

So what is happening? It would appear that when students watched videos that present a clear description of the scientific principles the student subsumed the content into their present construct. This would be fine if the currently held construct were accurate. However it is a no-win situation because if the construct is accurate then the student is learning little, if anything at all and the content is adding little to their cognitive development. However where the construct is flawed the student often did not engage with any learning as they did not "hear" the new concepts believing their current construct to be sufficient and correct. Muller's misconception videos were effective because they placed a sense of "confusion" into the learning forcing children to think more deeply. Indeed in interviews afterwards those who watched the latter videos scored one point higher in terms of "mental effort" expended than those using the Khan Academy videos.

There are many lessons to be drawn from this research but one is that this principle of using misconception is very powerful in subjects that are linear in their development. By this I mean where the learning of a new concept is built on a full understanding of one learnt earlier. For instance you are not going to understand equivalent fractions if your understanding of fractions themselves is not secure. Mathematics and Science are two such subjects that would benefit greatly from having previous constructs challenged heavily to ensure cognitive progression through the curriculum.

Similarly it means we should welcome misconceptions into the classroom. For the child proposing them there is an obvious learning element that needs to take place to correct their thinking, but what that particular child is unwittingly doing is presenting an element of cognitive dissonance to those who feel secure in the concept. The element of reasoning and dialogue around such debate is vital in gaining a full understanding for both groups of children. In defence of my lesson that started this debate I did allow the misconception of the numerator to be brought into the class discussion it was just that in my own mind I allowed it to remain there too long... but there again, maybe not, in hindsight!

Interestingly enough I decided to take a look at one of these legendary Khan videos (they are freely available on You Tube) and so as to keep the theme of this article cogent I looked at their video on the addition of fractions. I was intrigued that within ten seconds of the video the voice over commentary proudly declared *"Let's start with something which I hope won't confuse you too much"* and *"there* (as Shakespeare once said) *is the rub"*

Although the point has been made that Muller's work is more powerfully demonstrated in subjects where the concepts are linear we can broaden our thinking out from specific curriculum subjects and apply it to the mind in general. Simone Ritter of Radboud University Nijmegen in the Netherlands undertook a series of experiments to demonstrate the principle of, what she termed "Functional Fixedness" The process where the brain remains closed to new ideas because schemas are well entrenched and perceived to be secure in the mind of the participant. She got students to make a chocolate chip sandwich (a key element of the traditional Dutch breakfast). However they were asked to follow a series of instructions, the first of which involved pouring the chocolate chips onto a plate. At this point the subject underwent a process of, what Ritter describes as, "schema violation" i.e. where the task felt unnatural to the mind. From there they were asked to butter the bread and then turning it face down rub the chocolate chips onto the bread. In essence the subject ended up with an identical sandwich to that which they might have made using their own method but it was simply constructed in a counter-intuitive manner. The interesting thing is that subjects who undertook the sandwich task scored 15% higher in their ability to take on new learning in tasks set immediately after. It is as if the brain becomes attuned to dissonant thinking and the more it lives in this environment the more capable it seems to be of taking on new concepts and new learning.

Implications for Classroom Practice

The implications of this upon classroom teaching are readily evident. Whilst we all acknowledge that children are here to learn and take concepts on board there is something deep in the psyche of many us in the teaching profession that holds to the notion that it is the teacher that should chart a clear, simple and cognitive path through to understanding for the child. Traditionally this belief stemmed from the fact that the child would ultimately be presented with an activity or worksheet at the end of the lesson which sought to demonstrate that they had "learnt" what had been taught. The focus in this form of learning tends to be on keeping confusion to a minimum so that the child can achieve the designated task; this in turn becomes the ultimate destination on the learning journey. The flaw in this approach is that the end goal drives the learning down a very narrow and restrictive path and can, often unwittingly, prevent a deep engagement with the concept and even worse drive misconceptions deeper into the mind of the child.

Counter to this approach would be one that focuses on nurturing the fullest and richest understanding of the mathematical concept being taught. With this emphasis the lesson is likely to meander and morph through a series of conceptual frameworks as children journey with their own thinking. The teacher should ensure that at each point concepts are challenged rigorously and robustly even if this creates an element of dissonance or "confusion" because in this the child's mind will be challenged to drive out misconceptions and build up fresh constructs for themselves.

Here is one of the key features of teaching through dissonance. Whilst I wish I could claim that this knowledge came from a higher level order thinking process on my part rather a conclusion drawn from a lesson that sunk without trace, the truth is that creating dissonance in lessons causes children to expend more energy in the learning. Again whilst I am in no way advocating a passive teacher role what was very evident even in my original lesson was that the children were working harder to reach a point of understanding; the energy they expended served them well in developing fresh constructs. As someone once said the classroom is the only place where 30 people turn up to watch an adult at work and it is well documented that too many classes are dominated by the voice of the teacher rather than the voice of the learner but teaching through dissonance provides the perfect environment where children can reason, dialogue and challenge their own pre-conceptions.

WHAT'S WRONG WITH PENCILS ON THE FLOOR?

Classroom Climate and the Power of Environment

At the turn of this century the government commissioned Hay McBer to undertake a study that sought to elucidate the characteristics that were consistent in teachers who were deemed to be effective. They drew the conclusion that there were three key factors. They classed two; Teaching Skills and Professional Characteristics as input measures in the sense that they reflect what the teacher brings to the job and thereby what they "input" into the classroom. The third; Classroom Climate was categorised as an output measure because the data collated for this part of the research came from the end users (the children) and reflected their view of the class and the quality of the learning experience. The latter of the three is the most fascinating as it has built within it a complexity that is not easy to articulate. We will know from our own experience that within the heart of any organisation there exists an ethos and a culture that determines how people act and behave but seeking to define how this occurs is another matter altogether . Whilst I might agree with Hay McBer that if their data is drawn from children then it is an output measure, we need also to appreciate that the teacher is the key player in creating the classroom culture and the climate in the first place. Therefore teachers need to determine what they can "input" into their daily teaching and classroom practice that will deliver effective "output" scores in terms of classroom climate.

In my mind attention to the environment is the foundation block for establishing a clear learning culture that everything else builds upon. It sends out powerful hidden messages to children (and to visiting adults) about what is valued and the wider ethos of the school. Applying for deputy headships some years ago I was unable to visit easily in term time and being out of area and with no knowledge of the schools I travelled up to visit them both. Bearing in mind that the only access I had was to walk around the outside of the building and look in through the windows of a few classes (you could do that in those days!) I came away secure in the knowledge that I would be applying for one and not the other. What is it that had informed my decision? I cannot remember the specific details but quite simply one environment had left me with a buzz and a sense of a school that had a heart for learning and a love of children whilst the other left me feeling rather cold and ambivalent.

I would therefore concur with the DFE who not only devoted a whole section to The Physical Environment in the Excellence and Enjoyment training materials but wrote the following; *"The physical environment has a significant influence on learning. It gives children clear messages about how we value them and how we value learning"* (Part 3 p 56)

Whilst this might be difficult to prove empirically, we would probably all agree that we intrinsically know this to be right. Why is it that the sea view rooms in hotels, can command a premium price if environment has no impact? Why is that cities and towns spend vast amounts of taxpayer's money clearing litter and planting flowers to enter the Britain in Bloom competition if environment is of no consequence? We know in our hearts that the surroundings in which we work are vitally important and therefore we should not underestimate its impact on children. It is no surprise that

"Educational psychologists have found that environment can have a large impact on children's learning. There are classrooms that alienate children and those that engage them, and much research shows that children who feel engaged in their classroom are more receptive." (www.Teachernet "Classroom Displays") And so as Jane McGregor points out; *"research demonstrates that the learning environment affects the engagement, motivation, self-esteem, attendance, wellbeing and achievement of students" (Understanding and Managing Classroom Space)*

The original Hay McBer study sought to quantify the impact of environment on children's learning. They found that *"Pupil progress data for students from the primary classes in the classroom climate study correlated strongly with overall classroom climate (r = .51, p < .01)... This suggests that a pleasant physical environment combined with a lack of disruption is particularly important for academic progress in primary schools." (Teacher Effectiveness p30)*

Another more recent study published by Peter Barrett, a professor at Salford University found that *"a full 73 percent of the variation in pupil performance driven at the class level can be explained by the building environment factors."* Their data showed *that "all other things being equal, a child in the best environment could be expected to make two sub-levels more progress during a school year than an equivalent child in the "poorest" classroom environment. That equates to a whole year's average improvement for a child in reading, writing and maths" (quote from The Guardian 25th April 2013)* I appreciate that schools are not one dimensional and therefore there will never be a state where "all things being equal" can possibly apply but the study would certainly appear to confirm that environment plays a crucial role in enhancing academic progress, which is what we might intuitively expect.

How can the environment be such a powerful factor?

In his book The Tipping Point, Malcolm Gladwell makes reference to the "Broken Window Theory". This theory was first proposed by Philip Zimbardo in 1969 a psychologist from Stanford who undertook a very simple experiment. He arranged for a car with no number plates and the bonnet left open to be placed in The Bronx area of New York. He then left a second car in the same condition in Palo Alto, California. The car in the Bronx was attacked by vandals within minutes and within 24 hours anything of any value had been stripped from the car, all the windows were smashed, the upholstery torn and children were using it as a playground. The car in Palo Alto sat untouched for a week. At which point Zimbardo smashed one of the windows with a sledge hammer, soon after people joined in the car's destruction until, as in the Bronx, nothing of value was left. Zimbardo was interested to note that the majority of the "vandals" were *primarily well dressed, clean-cut and respectable citizens*" The thinking behind the "Broken Windows" theory is simply that the broken window gave off a hidden (or indeed, not so hidden) message that "no-one cares". It is vital to note that one simple change in the environment, the smashing of one window, sent off a powerful subliminal message to those in the community. The key is that *"it is not so much the actual broken window that is important, but rather the message the people receive from the broken window." (Wikipedia – Broken Windows Theory)*

In 1980 George Kelling was hired by the New York Transit company to tackle the wave of crime that existed on the city's subways. An exponent of the Broken Windows theory he chose to transform the situation through transforming the environment. There were regular outbreaks of graffiti on the subway trains on a virtual daily basis, so Kelling, and a man called David Gunn who was director of the system, believed the graffiti was sending out a broken window message. They vowed to rid all trains of graffiti and this they did with remarkably good effect. They built cleaning yards at the end of the line and as fast as the graffiti vandals struck the cleaners would move in, erasing their work. Gradually they noted a decline in subway crime.

In truth they used other strategies in conjunction with this but again rather than going for the more obvious issues of knife crime and tackling it head on they chose a "micro-scale broken window" and brought in a zero tolerance approach to petty fare dodging. Once again a clear message was sent out to the community. In the arresting of fare dodgers the police found that one in seven of them had an outstanding warrant for a previous crime and one in twenty were carrying a weapon. For the police it was a win-win situation; the environment was being transformed, they were shifting the culture in people's minds through the targeting of a relatively minor criminal act but at the same time were arresting key criminals in the community. As Galdwell points out; *"after a while the bad guys wised up, and began to leave their weapons at home and pay their fares."* However the starting point was the simple decision to change one factor within the environment and paint the subway trains.

Gladwell also goes on to point out something more pertinent to our discussion when he states; *"Broken Windows theory is based upon the premise that an epidemic can be reversed, can be tipped, by tinkering with the smallest details of the immediate environment" (Gladwell, 2000, p. 146).* Or to make the link between New York subways and classrooms crystal clear, when secondary school children were asked how they knew which teacher to play up in class one of the key factors that determined their behaviour was the state of the teacher's desk. We need to be mindful therefore of the impact that the environment has on children and robustly critique the quality of the classrooms in which we teach, lest we give children the wrong message and develop a classroom culture which hinders rather than assists learning.

Broken Windows Theory in Schools

They say if you want to find out what a man believes look at his bookcase and see what he reads. In many ways the bookcase can be a touchstone for the classroom as well. In my current role I get to visit plenty of schools and bizarrely you can tell a lot about a school from its bookcases. Those that have books falling off the shelves, with books laid on top of other books, some with ripped covers, others with pages falling out, give the visitor a clear impression of the school and the culture it will establish. As with Gladwell's broken window it presents an attitude that "no-one cares". This may not be intentional but it is a powerful statement. Those children sitting in the class imbibing the message of the environment who are then asked to "write neatly in their books" will sense the incongruity. Will they write neatly? It is unlikely because everything about the class is screaming out the opposite. The teacher is saying one thing with their lips and another in their action and sadly "actions always speak louder than words" Effective learning does not occur in arenas of dissonance and if the teacher wants the children to produce work of high quality then maybe the place to start is to look critically at the quality of display around the classroom. The values that the teacher communicates through their work in this area will speak volumes to children compared with a lengthy and comprehensive explanation of the virtues of working neatly in exercise books.

The belief that the bookcase has the potential to undermine all the good work that the teachers plans for in the class is taken up by Bruton and Thornton who implore teachers to *"Get rid of everything which is broken, has pieces missing, or is worn and looks tatty. Although this may seem ruthless, remember it is impossible to create an ethos of respect for resources if they are in a poor state of repair and appear 'unloved' (High-quality environments for learning, Pat Brunton and Linda Thornton)*

So is it true that; *"to ignore one piece of trash on the floor. . .one shirt improperly tucked in, one fight between kids, one bit of foul language, would send a disastrous no-one-cares message" (No Excuses, Thernstrom and Thernstrom, 2003)* or is this just the product of a teacher exhibiting early symptoms of OCD? The broken window theory would tend to imply that the environment around which you wrap each lesson is a greater determining factor than many of us have maybe appreciated.

Using the Environment to drive Classroom Culture

The concept of culture and how it roots itself deeply into any given organisation is complex but one thing is certain it is the way the ethos is lived out which is the determining factor rather than what is stated in documents, policies or spouted out in school assemblies. The truth is *"we set standards by the environment we offer to children" (Dean, 2001, p.197).* A well cared for and attractive environment sends powerful messages about expectations, and will therefore be *"a potent influence on how well students achieve a range of desired educational outcomes" (Fraser, 1986, p.182).*

So the child who arrives in a classroom on the first day of the autumn term to find half of the display boards empty and the rest filled with work left over from the previous term, will quickly draw conclusions about the teacher's values and their expectations. The class settles, the first register is read and the teacher sits the children down to explain the ethos of the class and his expectations of the children throughout the year. Sadly the child has determined the ethos already imbibing it from the environment around him which makes a more powerful statement than a few mealy mouthed clichés from the teacher. I describe such rooms as "Educational Warehouses" and to state the obvious they are not conducive to quality teaching. Conversely displays can be a powerful driver in establishing a rich culture of learning because *"Using visual displays in classrooms breeds success because 'students are provided with specific examples of how success is obtained" (The effect of the physical environment on teaching and learning Culp, B 2006:14).*

In similar vein to the McBer study Stephen Plank from Johns Hopkins University sought to determine the degree to which the physical appearance of the school and the classroom setting impacted upon learners. He concluded that whilst *"Fixing broken windows and attending to the physical appearance of a school cannot alone guarantee productive teaching and learning, ignoring them greatly increases the chances of a troubling downward spiral."(An Application of the Broken Windows Theory, S Plank, 2009)*

Working Walls or Curriculum Displays? – "Ownership" power

I know the current trend is to establish working walls within each class and whilst I recognise they may have a place in the primary classroom I personally am not a great lover of them. There are a range of reasons behind this. One of them is simply that they give the message that the only thing schools are for is to learn, learn, learn, in the narrowest of academic senses and I would hold to the view that schools are so much more than that and should be communities built around the warmth and nurture of a caring, compassionate classteacher. They should be a place where children feel free to be themselves and enjoy themselves in every area of school life. So whilst the display board that has the 6x table on it may have a slight subliminal impact on one area of learning if I was a child I would be far more captivated by a display that through flair and imagination captured my interest in a topic such as the Romans, Space or animals. The children in one of our classes created films based on Doctor Who to study history. At the outset the whole back wall of the classroom had a 3-D life size tardis in amongst other memorabilia relating to the programme later. For me such a display presents learning as vibrant, and fun, I am not convinced a Maths poster has the same effect. What I am saying is that certain displays give off subliminal messages to children whilst others create a different feel within the classroom. The power of this should not be underestimated.

Related to this is the children's need to gain ownership of the environment in which they work. The displays need to captivate, inspire and engage the children. It is not uncommon for our Year 6 class to be split into groups and for the children to design their own project displays using success criteria given to them by the display co-ordinator who then uses these to assess their final product. Beadle 2010, p.177) states that when children are involved in designing and putting up the displays, *'it gives the students a real sense of ownership of the classroom in which they are taught, and this being so, they will be more likely to respect not just the school fabric, but also the learning that takes place in the room they have ownership over.'* I appreciate that for younger children this approach may not be so readily accessible but the principle remains that children should take ownership of the environment themselves.

Partly related to this is some research that argued that when children's artwork actually incorporated into the fabric of the school with a sense of permanence e.g. through extensive tiled murals, *"children were considerably more positive about the school, compared to pupils in a control school."* The study admitted to only showing a correlation, not a causal link but again intuitively one feels there may be truth held within it. (Killeen et al, 2003)

Instilling Culture

If we accept, that the untidy bookcase and *"one piece of trash on the floor"* (see above) are not just small elements of untidiness but potentially powerful cultural messages writ large across our class then how should we resolve this? The teacher could stay behind after school and clear up but how does this drive the culture for the children? All the research points to the fact that the power of culture is held within ownership and it is therefore vital that the teacher ensures that the children become part of the environment culture themselves. The bookcase is "our" bookcase not only for us to use this year but it is a bookcase that others will use in the years after us, so why would we not wish to look after the books upon it? The reality is that this path develops in children a respect for others, a respect for property which in turn will have an impact on learning. If I am caring for the classroom why would I not care about the quality of my work and its presentation? Similarly when the teacher moves on to teach a lesson on caring for the planet for the sake of future generations it will have congruency because "caring for things" is part of "what we do as a class"; it is just that caring for a planet is an extension of this on a macro scale of global awareness rather than the micro scale of the class bookcase.

The problem with culture is that every classroom has one. You don't need to understand the principles of how it works. Just by turning up and being there every teacher will instil tacitly his or her own statement of values on the children they teach. However for those aware of its power there is the opportunity to use their knowledge to good effect. It might help if we understood a little of how culture operates and gathers momentum within an organisation or a group of people.

Psychologists have long recognised that "conformity" is a key feature of human behaviour. As David Straker points out; *"We are a tribal animal, which leads us to have a deep need to belong to a group of some sort. Conforming to group norms is a signal to the other group members that 'I am like you."* The desire to conform has a profound effect on both our thinking and our behaviour.

Solomon Asch was a pioneer in the field of social psychology and undertook some ground breaking research in the 1950's. The study focused on a vision test. Groups of students were shown a series of diagrams similar to the one on the right. They were then asked which of the lines; A, B or C were identical in size to the line in the left. They were asked to answer the question out loud to the whole group in turn. However only one member of the group was a true participant the remainder were actors. Asch always ensured that the true participant was asked last. Prior to this the "actors" proceeded to deliver false answers that were then substantiated by the others in the group.

What Asch found was that 75% of the participants gave an incorrect answer to at least one of the questions. Only 25% were willing to "go it alone" and answer all the questions correctly standing against the pressure to conform to the views of their peers. The experiment has been replicated in a variety of contexts and settings[3] but consistently the scores demonstrate that a high percentage of those taking part will defy their own intelligence to conform to the group.

These findings have powerful implications for those who work intrinsically with others in social situations. For instance, research has been found that placing a message such as *"Do not speed"* on a road is not as effective as a sign that says *"98.5% of drivers drove below 30 mph in this zone last month"*. The latter statement taps into people's deep need to be part of a group and to conform to what they believe is the social norm in a particular area, in this instance, the speed of their car. It also explains why a lady in a waiting room sat for an inordinate amount of time, even though she had heard the fire alarm sound, saw (what she thought) was smoke billowing out from under the door and could hear people seemingly evacuating the building in the adjacent rooms. What made her remain rooted to her chair for a length of time that put her life in danger? The simple fact that everyone else in the room (actors in on the event) ignored the warnings and remained reading their newspapers and working on their laptops.

---

[3] One of the most bizarre is the people in the lifts which can be found at the following web address
http://www.youtube.com/watch?feature=player_embedded&v=uuvGh_n3I_M

As a classroom is a highly social setting the ramifications of this research for the teacher are profound. For instance it probably goes a long way to explaining why many more able children seek to mask their ability, even deliberately seeking to underachieve so that they can remain within the social realm of their peers. However the classroom environment also impinges on this in a major way. When a teacher sets up a room with vibrant, clear displays, provides materials of a high quality for children to use and all the while encourages them to value and care for the classroom environment, they are not just creating an aesthetic base for the children to work in. They are delivering a very powerful cultural message to the children that "this is the way we do things around here". They are laying down social markers that will underpin what the class comes to believe and accept as their cultural norm and once this occurs the "conformity principle" will take hold and they will subliminally start to follow the social expectation set for them as a group.

I often hear teachers bewailing the fact that the children don't care for the room, the resources and at times even each other. If this is the case, then apply the "broken window" theory to your classroom and seek to elucidate where the children are getting these messages from. We cannot expect children to put pencils back in pencil pots if we leave coffee mugs on a classroom display. We cannot ask children to clear away at the end of the lesson, if some of the artefacts from yesterday's Science lesson remain piled up by the door waiting to be returned to the resources room. The reality is that in such instances the children will conform to what they see as the norm in practice rather than the norm in principle.

Conclusion

This brings us full circle to where we started in this article, with the principle of classroom culture. This is a vast topic but when limited to just the area of environment, it becomes clear that teachers set the culture wittingly or unwittingly, for the children. The environment is a powerful driver; as it sets the tone and is the visual backdrop for all the learning that is undertaken in the class.

I am always irritated by the fact that there is usually someone who somehow manages to articulate all that needs to be said in one succinct sentence and so it is in this case. I will therefore leave the last word to Malaguzzi, founder of the Regio Emilia schools, who wrote; *'Education must come to be recognised as the product of complex interactions, many of which can be realised when the environment is a fully participating element.' (Malaguzzi, L, 1998 'History, Ideas and Basic Philosophy')*

SELF ESTEEM – WHAT IS IT REALLY?

Preface

For as long as I can remember I held to the traditional notion that for children to thrive in life they needed to be shielded both from failure and from the impact this supposedly had on their self-esteem. The mantra ran that if we focused on a child's area of perceived weakness the resultant dip in confidence would leave them bereft of the ability to tackle any task they deemed difficult. Two things came to challenge and ultimately change my thinking in this regard. Firstly I appointed a new deputy and secondly I stumbled across the work of Carol Dweck.

Working with the Year 6 Class

I appointed Jon Westwood to the staff in 2004 and he has worked here as the Deputy and Year 6 teacher since that time. In 2009 Ofsted arrived and whilst they noted that the teaching was outstanding throughout the school they felt compelled to comment that; Teaching is especially effective in Year 6. However it wasn't simply the quality of Jon's teaching that caused me to rethink through the issue of self-esteem. The challenge came from watching a quality classroom practitioner produce standards of work from children that set new benchmarks and yet seemingly with little regard to the traditional view of protecting children's self-esteem. Needless to say I was intrigued!

The first thing to say about Jon is that his relationships with children are exceptional and there is a real respect and warmth about everything he does. They respond in kind and truly enjoy working with him. This is the basis upon which everything else in Jon's class is built, and it is this element that forms the foundation on which the argument spelt out below is built. The aspect that interests me most about Jon's teaching style is that he is not afraid to "tell it like it is". If he feels a child is not performing to the best of their ability, or that a piece of work is not up to the standard he would expect then he is never reticent in making his feelings known. He is never sharp with any child, never raises his voice he just points out to them that he feels they are underperforming. I have observed him on many occasions informing a child that the piece of literacy they have produced was "pants" and yet bizarrely by the end of the year the children appear to have grown in confidence and their attainment has rocketed. So with my traditional views on self-esteem seemingly in shreds I decided to interview the children one at a time to get their take on Jon's approach and it was this that opened my eyes to a brave new world.

The children were more than happy to spill the beans on their teacher's style of classroom management. There was a general acceptance from all the children that Mr Westwood's style was more direct than other teachers. *"If your work is pants he will tell you"* one girl proudly informed me and they all noted the same. However it was their reaction to this methodology that transformed my own standpoint. One boy articulated what appeared to be the general consensus within the class when he said *"If he tells you that you can do better this means he believes you can and he expects you to achieve even more than you have and that makes you feel good about yourself. If teachers always tell you your work is good then you feel like you can't do better but here you can do more. You could become the best in the class"* None of the children appeared to be phased by the apparent "criticism" In fact they had turned it on its head and saw it in a highly positive light. They felt intrinsically that no teacher would ask a child to do something they could not achieve and thus the challenge to better themselves came across as a message of affirmation to the child that Jon believed in them as learners and this in turn inspired them to achieve more. As another boy said *"If he tells you your work is pants then it means that he thinks you can do better, he has faith in you and believes you can work to a high standard and that makes me feel good about myself"*

My head was reeling from the simplicity with which they expressed their views. They appeared to have taken the self-esteem debate turned it inside out and upside down and left me with the feeling that my traditional "Candy Floss" view of self-esteem was left very wanting. We appeared to have children believing they could achieve more than they had before and some believing they could (apparently) *"become the best in the class"* They all seemed to respond positively and as one child put it; *"I like it because it makes you feel you can do better, he believes in you and he thinks you can do it."* It should not have escaped anyone's notice that the underpinning for all this hinges on Jon's relationship with the children and their respect for him, without this the whole process would unravel very quickly but the power and effectiveness of the feedback being given was seemingly undisputable. Far from feeling deflated by the seeming criticism one boy stated that *"When you are told it is wrong it makes you feel good about yourself because it makes you feel like you can do even better"* I found the whole thing totally counter intuitive; how could a child claim that *"when you are told it is wrong it makes you feel good about yourself"* Yet I could see their point of view and could appreciate what Jon was doing for them.

What was more interesting was the children's articulation of how this approach was changing the learning culture within the classroom as a whole. The children were almost contemptuous about experiences in previous classes (probably mine!) where the teacher always looked for a positive slant on their work. One boy said *"Some teachers say that work is good when it isn't and that makes me feel weird"* He articulated how he felt a real sense of dissonance when a teacher made an encouraging comment about work he either believed was not his best or work where he knew he had not totally applied himself. He went on to say *"Also if they say it is good then you wouldn't try harder next time because you have reached the standard. In fact when they say it is good and I know it isn't it makes me feel like they have not read it properly and that they don't care much"* It was in statements like this that I could see how Jon's philosophy was driving such a strong culture of achievement into the children in his class. Some expressed thoughts in terms of the teacher simply raising expectations *"It makes us work harder the next time because we know what the expectations are and if we don't want to have to do it again we know what to avoid"* but others attached this raising of the bar to their own intrinsic development as learners *"Being criticised feels OK because I know he thought I could do better."* The simple truth was expressed by one girl who said; *"If the teacher says your work is good all the time it stops you trying harder"*

The children were also very cognisant of the fact that it was the quality of the teacher's feedback that enabled their learning to move forward. One child commented that "There is no point telling you that your work is pants and then not telling you how to improve it, so he always tells you what is wrong with it and what you can do to make it better". As John Hattie has found in his meta-analysis of what contributes to quality learning, one of the key features is the quality of feedback that children receive from their teacher. So we have ended up with a class that has the most robust comments I have witnessed and yet children who appear to be emotionally thriving in a culture that raises standards and drives children's desire to learn forward apace.

The power of this fundamental shift in thinking was clearly illustrated late one afternoon. As the children were completing a writing task, one of the girls called Jon over to look at her work. At the end of a long day Jon sped read the work and told her it was fine. As he turned to move away he felt a tug on his shirt and he heard the girl say "Now read it again and tell me what I need to do to improve it" To have children pro-actively seeking out "criticism" of their work so they can improve it has to be one of the most powerful drivers in any learning culture.

Carol Dweck's work on Mindsets

It was around this time that Carol Dweck published her work on Mindsets and upon reading it I suddenly found that someone had developed a framework into which my new thinking on self-esteem fitted seamlessly. There have always been subtle clues that the traditional view of self-esteem that sought to shield children from failure was somewhat flawed. For example, if this were the case then one might expect that secure self-esteem would reside in all the high achievers and low self-esteem would inflict those who were more academically challenged. However any teacher will tell you issues of self-esteem span the complete ability range.

The crux of Dweck's work focused not on the child's ability but on how the child perceived themselves in terms of their learning. She developed the dual concepts of "Fixed" and "Growth" mindsets.

Those with a Fixed Mindset held the view that intelligence was inherently innate and that no amount of work or effort would alleviate your ability to succeed. So if presented with an activity that presented any form of challenge would readily conclude that their failure to achieve was due to their lack of natural ability. Children with this mindset quickly became victims of "learned helplessness" as they limited their potential to learn anything that offers any sense of challenge.

Those with a Growth Mindset on the other hand saw challenge as an opportunity to "give it a go". They viewed learning as a process not a performance and therefore were able to see failure as a stepping stone in the learning process rather than an indictment on their innate ability. They developed tenacity in their learning, happily working in Vygotsky's "zone of proximal development" without any challenge to their perception of their own intelligence

Dweck concluded that children's perception of themselves and their personal view of their own self-esteem was not related to their ability but whether they saw their ability as fixed and a previously determined factor or one of unlimited potential to be explored. She noted that when children tackled a given task in school how they perceived it at the outset had a huge impact on their view on what might constitute success. Those children in a fixed mindset invariably saw every task through a "performance" lens, meaning they saw the task as one that needed to be completed successfully so as to confirm their own status of perceived ability. To fail would only confirm to them that "they weren't smart". They therefore held a natural preference for activities where they knew they would succeed because this would lead to their gaining approval and would shield them from what they perceive as any unwelcome assessment of their ability. Conversely the growth mindset children viewed tasks as an opportunity to learn. They were not deterred by whether they were successful in the ultimate sense of the word but held greater store on whether they had taken their own personal learning forward.

Dweck's research included a raft of experiments that substantiated her thinking. In one of them she used a questionnaire to divide children into those with fixed or growth mindsets. They were then given 12 mathematical problems to solve, 8 of which were relatively straightforward followed by 4 that were relatively unsolvable. As the children moved onto the complex questions those of a fixed mindset started to denigrate their own ability and lost interest in the difficult questions very early on. However those in the growth mindset continued to work seamlessly on the tasks and actually managing to solve some of the more complex questions. Just as poignant were the conclusions drawn from a debriefing afterwards. In this only a third of the fixed mindset children believed they would be able to successfully tackle the easy questions correctly if they tackled them again and whilst most had scored 8 correct answers they perceived their personal scores to be much lower. Whilst it would be unwise to draw sweeping conclusions from a single experiment (and Dweck doesn't, she has banks of similar data) it is easy to see that the fixed mindset undermines any construct of learning. As Guy Claxton once said "If you are not in the fog you are not learning". These children are prevented from entering the learning space, hampered by their desire to always be correct and to see every learning activity as an assessment of their ability rather than an opportunity to learn fresh concepts and develop new understanding.

No surprise then that when children with a fixed mindset were given the option of an easy task with little chance of making a mistake; a hard task but possible to achieve with some effort; or a hard task designed to expose children to a new concept 80% of them chose one of the first two. In fact 50% chose the easier of the two options. However in the growth mindset group over 60% chose the challenging task that offered the opportunity to learn. In similar vein the same children were asked if they would prefer to get a good grade in class or to do something that presented a challenge. 65% of those with the fixed mindset chose the good grade option whilst 68% of those with a growth mindset chose the opportunity to be challenged by a task. Without feeling the need to spell out the obvious it should be clearly evident to all that the fixed mindset legislates against learning in every context. It is a powerful disabler and if left unchecked will hinder a child's achievement throughout the entirety of their school life.

If you have followed the thread of Dweck's argument it will not surprise you to find that she has found that the most vulnerable students, who often crash and burn at some point are higher ability girls. They are those who have maybe never found any challenge in learning but often in adolescence or later at university they hit the brick wall of "failure" (or challenge as we might term it) for the first time. Unless they have been well schooled with a growth mindset this is often the time that the performance based culture they have lived in for so long leads them to conclude that they were not as intelligent as they first thought. If they stay in this mindset then their ability to continue learning will be ultimately undermined by their lack of understanding of Guy Claxton's fog.

It may well be argued that such students had never been placed in a meaningful, challenging, learning arena where they had the chance to taste seeming failure before experiencing that moment when the light dawns as understanding fills the mind. If it is true this is a sad indictment on schools and maybe Dweck is right when she says "Primary schools typically provide a low-key environment in which the work tends to be carefully paced and teachers try to keep failure to a minimum. However if vulnerable children do not encounter difficulty they will be greatly hampered in their achievement" (Mindset p 20)

My reception teacher once showed me a piece of writing from one of her pupils. It was an outstanding piece of writing for a child in their first year at school. I asked her what feedback she had given to the child. She replied "I told her to put it in the finished tray, well there is not a lot one can say when work is that good" That good? What does "that good" mean? Did the work contain a semi colon, an adverbial clause or the correct use of a hyphen? Whilst we should celebrate a child's success at every point in their educational life we should at the same time ensure that they are placed on the growth mindset road rather than leading them subliminally and in this instance unwittingly into a performance orientated culture. So feedback should be an elemental part of the learning experience for every child lest we end up unwittingly building into children the notion that for them performance is the end goal to all learning and of course it isn't it is about constantly moving forward.

Can a fixed mindset be redeemed?

Here lies the most crucial of questions for if the answer is not in the affirmative it would seem to infer that many children are condemned to a miserable existence of swimming against the tide of learning.

When I spoke earlier about my deputy's approach it will have become evident that his class and the ethos was singularly different from others in the school. At the time I was not fully conversant with Dweck's work and was struggling to understand why it was that children would gain a shot of confidence under Jon's tutelage. It became evident, although we did not have Dweck's framework to set it in at the time, that he was developing a growth mindset in his class. What was also apparent was that children were having their mindset transformed through his approach as they entered his class. Having followed through Dweck's work we have now fully embedded the principles underlying throughout the school, but those early days showed quite clearly that in the hands of a good classroom practioner it is possible to shift the mindsets of children quite substantially.

Dweck would argue the same, she remains convinced that change is possible and has been evidenced frequently in research. The one possible proviso being that the sooner a healthy mindset is developed the more effective and easier it will be. The issue is getting those who are the "significant others" in the life of a child to understand how the building of true self-esteem works.

One of the common misconceptions in both the minds of parents and teachers alike is that children need to be shielded from "harmful" challenging experiences which may lead to them "failing" and developing a low self-esteem. To counter this most people assume that whenever possible children should receive praise as the antidote to the feeling of failure. Indeed "85% of parents believe that praising a child's ability when they do well is something necessary for a child's self-esteem". This view "leads us as adults to lie to children – to exaggerate positives, to sugar coat negatives, or to hide negative information entirely. We fear that negative information and or criticism will damage self-esteem" (Mindset p127) Whilst there seems an initial logic behind this approach the reality is that it "instils in children a sense of "contingent self-worth" i.e. they feel worthy only when they succeed and feel worthless when they fail" Self-esteem is related more to resilience in tasks that offer challenge rather than finding ways to shore up and disguise apparent weaknesses a child may have. This would explain why after a classroom test when the children were asked to report their scores the growth mindset children reported them with 100% accuracy but 40% of the fixed mindset children exaggerated their marks. The reality being that for the latter group their "self-worth" was attached to their achievement and a deep need for approval whereas for the former it related more to their own passion for learning.

However if teachers share the power of the growth mindset with children it can shift their thinking substantially. At one point in her research Dweck shared two articles on the life of Albert Einstein. One emphasised the fact that he was able to achieve so much in the field of Science because he was naturally gifted. The other drew the conclusion that his success came through effort and hard work. In follow up tasks she found that "Students who read the fixed mindset theory passage were significantly more likely to select a performance based task" (Mindset p23) The key feature to draw from this is that if changes can be made in such a short space of time then there should certainly be the expectation that mindsets have the capacity to be challenged and changed. Aronson developed research amongst underachieving black Americans spending time working with them on mindset change. He likewise found that both their attainment and their enjoyment of school rose appreciably but more importantly the children's perception of themselves as academically orientated improved.

Is there ever a place for praising children? Of course there is and there will be plenty of opportunities for children with their teachers to step back from the incremental path of learning and relish the success achieved. However Dweck is clear that to praise attainment will drive the growth mindset deeper into the child and she therefore encourages teachers to praise the effort that lies behind the learning. This is not just semantics but is a powerful determinant as to which mindset we build within children. In a society that is essentially founded on meritocracy the path of least resistance is to believe that natural ability determines all. It is almost as if the process of effort itself is actively despised. It is why we tend to accept unquestioningly that the student who passes an exam whilst claiming not to revise is deemed to be naturally gifted and we celebrate, and are even proud of such a stance. If we are to counter this cultural backdrop then the message of the growth mindset needs to be spelt out loud and clear to children so that they can remain focused on the path of learning rather than the path of achieving. As Einstein said "Failure is success in progress" but few with the fixed mindset would accept this seeing failure as a blight on their own ability rather than a stepping stone to further greatness.

So whilst we know that David Beckham has a natural talent for sport we need to balance that with the view of his Manchester United manager Alex Ferguson who said; "David Beckham is Britain's finest striker of a football not because of God-given talent but because he practices with a relentless application that the vast majority of less gifted players wouldn't contemplate." It is all too easy to fall into the trap of writing off achievement with the broad brush stroke reason of innate ability. However as Jack Nicklaus (the golfer) said "Achievement is largely the product of steadily raising one's levels of aspiration and expectation" and a growth mindset allows that aspiration and expectation to grow. Each time we delve into the realm of successful achievement then Dweck's framework of mindsets seems to hold centre stage. So let's leave the last word to her; "The key to self-esteem does not relate to how confident one feels about oneself tackling a given task but rather your view of intelligence and whether it is fixed (therefore every task measures one's ability) or malleable (therefore every task has the ability to increase intelligence)"

IS GUIDED READING A FIGMENT OF THE LITERARY IMAGINATION?

Preface

The rationale for this article is predicated on the fact that Reading falls into two major areas. In the first instance children concentrate on *"Learning to read"* and use phonic skills and decoding strategies to make sense of print. The teaching at Key Stage 1 will tend to focus primarily in this area and more especially in the early years.

In succeeding years the emphasis shifts towards children *"Reading to learn"* and the teaching moves towards engaging children with the nuances of textual form and the study of literary conventions. The children will explore a given passage at a deeper level using skills like inference and deduction and might focus on how the writer has constructed the text to create a specific effect.

This article deals primarily with the second of these and whilst this might be considered to be the domain of the Key Stage 2 classes there are aspects which will be equally relevant to their Key Stage 1 counterparts.

Introduction

My starting point for engaging with the issue of Guided Reading centres around three issues all of which need to be addressed if we are to move on in this area.

1. Whilst the children engaged in the focus group of a class guided reading session may well be acquiring a quality experience driven by the teacher, my general feeling is that the learning undertaken by the groups working "independently" fails to attain to the same standard. Inspectors within the LA have commented that they have yet to see a Guided Reading session that would be judged above "satisfactory" in Ofsted terms and this is always due to the provision and the consequent learning made by those in the "independent groups. "A stance that Ofsted themselves observed and commented on in their report Reading for Pleasure and Purpose which states that *"It took too little account of the needs of other groups in the class and the tasks set for them lacked challenge. In some instances, pupils were left to their own devices to read silently or share books. Although some enjoyed the opportunity, others merely flicked through their books with little apparent interest."*

2. Secondly I am also concerned that much of what we have called "Guided Reading" is in fact a replication of what children undertake in their Literacy lessons when they deconstruct texts as part of the writing process. This duplication of learning has a bearing on the third issue which is...

3. Despite our best efforts the curriculum remains strongly weighted towards Numeracy and Literacy. This balance can become skewed and therefore unhealthy. I suspect that one solution may be to look at all the constituent parts of each subject and reflect on how they might be drawn together more holistically. This would prevent the undue repetition of the teaching of certain concepts and free up time to

develop a more broad and balanced curriculum. In that sense there is a need to "Work smarter, not harder."

Whilst these three issues were the starting point for my thinking, I found myself quickly engaging with the more fundamental question of *"What should we be trying to achieve in our Guided Reading sessions?"* This led back to various source documents such as the National Literacy Strategy but also, and more importantly, some of the writings that underpinned the rationale behind the introduction of Guided Reading.

What is the Philosophy behind Guided Reading?

Guided Reading was introduced as part of the National Literacy Strategy (1998) and was one of the focused tasks within the "Literacy Hour." It arose in response to a debate stimulated by an Ofsted report *(The Teaching of Reading in 45 Inner London Primary Schools, 1996)* which was highly critical of the universally accepted practice of listening to individual children read; saying it *'had become an unproductive routine exercise'*. Immediately following the publication of this report, the government established a Literacy Task Force, whose remit was to *develop 'a strategy for substantially raising standards of literacy in primary schools over a five to ten year period'*. Their work led to the development of the National Literacy Strategy.

Some years previous to this, the principles of Guided Reading were being pioneered by Myrtle Simpson, an inspector of schools, and Ruth Trevor, the National Adviser on Reading in New Zealand. Their work dovetailed into Barbara Rogoff's later work on "Guided Participation". Her theory whilst being Vygotskyan in origin and strongly rooted in his theory of Social Constructivism (that children create meaning in a social or group context), stated that Guided Participation involves an *"experienced people play a guiding role, facilitating learners' involvement and often participating alongside learners—indeed, often learning themselves."* For

Rogoff, the teacher plays the role of co-learner in the guided reading session modelling the process of learning and reading alongside the child. The key however, remains that the child constructs their own learning rather than a didactic form of teaching in a group setting.

As Rogoff states; "*child cognitive development is an apprenticeship-it occurs through guided participation in social activity with companions supporting and stretching both their understanding and skill in using the tools of culture". (Barbara Rogoff Apprenticeship in thinking 2000)* In the context of Guided Reading this is aptly summarised by Gavelek and Raphael who state *"This is a social constructivist" view of teaching. It involves the teacher making a shift from asking predetermined questions designed to ensure that the students arrive at the "right" meaning to facilitating conversations that encourage students' exploratory talk as they arrive at a deeper meaning (Gavelek and Raphael, 1996).*

From this pedagogical background the principles of Guided Reading were integrated into the Literacy Framework. To be fair, it was a philosophy the original Ofsted report pointed towards when the inspectors commented that '*effective teaching of pupils in groups and especially as a whole class, was uncommon*'

Its hinged not on the "teaching of reading" but on the teacher *"guiding the learners through the text by providing signposts to the most important and most helpful features of the textual landscape" (Guided Reading, Ins of Ed).* As Dowhower states; *"Guided Reading is specifically designed to enable comprehension strategies to be taught systematically and used by students across a range of texts. The emphasis is on silent reading because it is more authentic and relevant to real life than oral reading, and it is also more effective for learning than oral reading" (Dowhower, 1999; Quoted in The Guided Reading Approach p3)*

This is certainly true at KS2 where the National Literacy Strategy itself states that, *"The KS2 objectives are built on the understanding that pupils will have attained a basic level reading fluency." (NLS p7)* Hence Guided Reading beyond year 3 (and many children in year 2) is related to meaning and comprehension rather than the acquisition of the basic skills of decoding print. To this end the teaching of guided reading *"focuses on independent reading rather than modelling the process for pupils" (NLS p12)* and in the minds of those who wrote the document it *"takes the place of an individualised Reading Programme" (NLS p12).* This is in line with one of the main tenets of the National Curriculum which is that *"Reading is using a range of strategies to get to the meaning of the text. This principle is at the heart of the National Curriculum" (p3)*

It is probably true to say that many Guided Reading sessions throughout the country neither reflect the theory nor the pedagogy outlined above and the effectiveness of the learning has consequently been diluted and in most cases, has diminished markedly. For many teachers Guided Reading (apart from becoming a huge classroom management issue) has fallen into any or all of the following categories:

- Many Guided Reading sessions tend to be "led" rather than "facilitated" (using Rogoff's terminology) by the teacher. This results in an experience for the child where the ability to construct their own learning alongside their peers has been dismantled and a form of didactic teaching and prescriptive learning ensues. This is contrary to the key principle that underpins the "Guided Participation" philosophy of learning.
- This means the teacher takes on a very different role from "Reading Expert" As E. Lowe states when commenting on Rogoff's work *"Guided participation involves the bridging of different perspectives among the more and less experienced participants, and also the way each participant's involvement in the activity is structured."* The emphasis therefore is on drawing out the views of each child and melding them

into a coherent piece of learning on their behalf; in this sense it is the antithesis of the "top-down" model of teaching.

- The teacher may easily fall into the role of merely checking or testing comprehension after a text has been read by the student. As Dowhower (1999) reports, there is evidence that many teachers assume the role of interrogators because they tend to confuse assessment with the direct constructivist teaching of comprehension which is at the heart of the Guided Reading rationale.

- The session may also descend into "round robin" reading. This is in essence a return to individualised reading in a group setting. If a key area of the teaching of reading relates to the child's enjoyment of the text one might argue that a return to the child choosing their own book to read might be more beneficial.

- Furthermore as Ofsted stated in their report, *hearing* children read is not *teaching* them to read therefore this form of reading is only useful as a form of assessment as it does not in and of itself take the child forward in their learning. As the Institute of Education stated *"Hearing children read may be useful when assessing their reading skills but it is not a good way to teach reading" (Why use Guided Reading p4)*

- Where the teacher is aware that hearing is not the same as teaching they may be tempted to "teach" reading in this context, but this only returns us to the principles that the Ofsted report tried to steer us away from that this is just individualised reading in a group context and will *"become an unproductive routine exercise". (Ofsted 1996)*

- Interestingly enough Dowhower's (1999) research found that rather than round robin reading enhancing children's ability to comprehend the text *"oral round robin has been shown to decrease comprehension"(Quoted in The Guided Reading Approach p3)*

None of this takes the debate forward about what any school should do with regards to Guided Reading but it does confirm Ofsted's assertion that; *"Most schools use guided reading as one way of teaching reading. However, its quality in the ineffective schools was unsatisfactory in one third of lessons. Too many teachers did not understand its principles and struggled to teach it successfully." (Ofsted, 2004 p4)*

As the New Zealand government found when seeking to implement Guided Reading *"For guided reading to be used effectively, teachers need to be aware of and appreciate the basic understandings or underlying theoretical perspectives on which the approach is based. (The Guided Reading Approach p2)*

Therefore without a secure pedagogical underpinning it is not surprising that Guided Reading has morphed into something unrecognisable from its original pure philosophical state. If it is to return to classrooms effectively then teachers need to have a clear rationale and understanding as to the pedagogy before they seek to implement the teaching and learning practically in their classrooms.

So what is Guided Reading?

Beyond my own concerns relating to the imbalance in the curriculum and the quality of provision for those working "independently", I have growing issues with the whole concept of how Guided Reading has been rolled out. Indeed I am beginning to wonder whether it actually exists as a cogent concept in its current form (hence the title). My premise for this would be as follows:

Current Practice in School

If Guided Reading is the means through which children are introduced to the *"features of the textual landscape" (Institute of Education)* then much of what we are teaching in these lessons tends to skew towards textual de-construction, as opposed to pure reading. The focus of the lesson hinges around introducing children to textual forms and conventions in a range of genres. I was surprised when questioning staff with regard to the content of our own guided reading sessions a few years ago how much of the KS1 programme centres on this theme. I had assumed that whilst in KS2 the children might be "Reading to Learn" that the focus in KS1 would be more rooted in "Learning to Read" but this is often not the case. Whilst these approaches to Guided Reading are philosophically pure and I have no qualms about the quality of the learning experience being offered, it does leave us with some interesting points to ponder.

Texts in isolation

I am finding myself increasingly challenged by the fact that Guided Reading is being taught in a separate lesson, often with a text which is not related to the work the children are undertaking in the class as a whole. The session appears to stand alone as a seeming "bolt on" activity within the school day. One of the major criticisms of the curriculum nationally is that it has become too disparate and lacks cohesion in its delivery therefore I do find it somewhat baffling as to why we might study a text in relative isolation from the rest of the child's learning.

Connection and Repetition

Related to the above, as well as to the debate on curriculum balance, is my observation whilst in classes that often the morning literacy lesson includes a quality textual analysis with the whole class. However in the afternoon the same children are sitting in a Guided Reading group, studying virtually an identical skill set using a text (often) unrelated to anything else they are learning. Apart from the fact that this approach will create an obvious imbalance towards Literacy within the timetable, it also lacks any coherent joined up thinking with regards to the curriculum as a whole. I know one of the reposts to this argument will be; that in the Guided Reading session the children have access to differentiated texts. This is true and may add something to a child's experience but if this is the case why when we undertake the same activity in the Literacy lesson do we not feel the same need to differentiate the texts used? I appreciate that on occasions teachers do differentiate texts but this only leads to the conclusion that the later lesson is a direct mirror of the one undertaken earlier. Leaving this aside, this does not get round the fact that the text in the literacy lesson is likely to be embedded in the holistic curriculum whilst that in the Guided Reading session is likely to remain as a stand-alone activity.

Curriculum Richness

The truth is, if we wish to deconstruct texts they are best done in the context of a cohesive piece of learning. The English National Curriculum at KS2 states that children should; *"distinguish between fact and opinion [for example, by looking at the purpose of the text, the reliability of information]" (En 2 KS2 3f).* Whilst this is a worthy goal and highly relevant to a child's reading progress it seems incongruous to undertake an activity related to this and then to move into a History lesson where the learning objective taken from the National Curriculum might be *"Pupils should be taught to recognise that the past is represented and interpreted in different ways, and to give reasons for this."(History Ks2 3a).*

This not only overloads the curriculum with literacy but the latter lesson will be much richer than the former being set in the context of the historical learning for that term. This scenario can be replicated throughout the Reading element of the National Curriculum. Why are we teaching *"skimming and scanning" (Eng 2 KS2 3a,b)* in Guided Reading when it can be taught in a Science lesson when finding out information for a project on invertebrates. Again why read an article in Guided Reading seeking to *"consider an argument critically" (Eng 2 KS2 3g)* when in the Geography lesson the children are studying a piece on Climate Change. Similarly at KS1 the obvious time to show children a contents page is in a Science lesson when they need it not in an unrelated Guided Reading activity designed for the purpose.

Is Guided Reading actually Guided Writing?

One of the conclusions I have drawn since embarking on this journey is that we need to be quite clear as to what we feel Guided Reading is seeking to achieve. For many, Guided Reading has become a confusing activity with many using it to assess reading rather than teach it, or to simply provide an opportunity for the teacher to "teach" children how a contents page works or other literary conventions.

However, reading should in essence be a pleasurable experience for the child. Most of us in our adult life read solely for pleasure. We either read fiction because we wish to get lost in the narrative of a good story, or we read non-fiction because we find the subject matter engaging and stimulating. Interesting to note therefore, that when Ofsted were commissioned to evaluate the teaching of reading in primary schools they entitled their report "Reading for purpose *and* pleasure" (their emphasis not mine).

It is no secret that my favourite story of all time is "The Lion, the Witch and the Wardrobe" I have read the book on numerous occasions to children and love the story held within its pages. As an adult I appreciate the allegory within the story which adds a depth of meaning and the nuances relating to this throughout the text add to my enjoyment of the story as a whole. The book contains magical pieces of writing none more so than Mrs Beaver explaining Aslan to the children;

'If there's anyone who can appear before Aslan without their knees knocking, they're either braver than me or else just silly.'
'Then he isn't safe?' asked Lucy
Safe?' said Mr. Beaver. 'Don't you hear what Mrs. Beaver tells you? Who said anything about safe? 'Course he isn't safe. But he's good. He's the King, I tell you

It is a masterful piece of writing in my opinion, with its clever juxtaposition of the words "safe" and "good". However if you asked me if I would like to deconstruct this particular passage and look at the use of adjectives used within it, or whether I would like to look at CS Lewis' use of short sentences then the answer is a resounding... No. My preference both as an adult and a child would be to read on and enjoy the story, anything less than that would break the continuity of the narrative, diminishing the pleasure of the story. It is little wonder that children are in danger of losing their love of reading. *(See below – Children's love of literature)*

Does this mean that textual analysis is wrong? Not necessarily.

Whilst I would not wish to study every nuance of the grammar and the syntax held within the text I might happily embark on a conversation with anyone about the macro elements within the book. For instance: What impact does the Turkish Delight have on Edmund's character? What is the deep magic and why was it necessary? These questions might (and probably would) add to my enjoyment of the story and therefore my enjoyment of the book as a whole. But is this not why many adults attend book clubs?

However the major purpose for deconstructing the text would not be if I wanted to *read* The Lion, The Witch and the Wardrobe, but if I wished to *write* a book in a similar genre. When I look at it dispassionately most of our Guided Reading sessions are actually assisting children's ability to *write* rather then their ability to *read*. Whilst no child would wish to deconstruct the story for the purposes of reading their engagement heightens considerably when placed in the context of writing. From this standpoint the child seeking to write a quality piece of literature is using the text as a model for their own work. The narrative (and the consequent enjoyment that narrative brings) now switches from the pages of the text to the mind of the child. They now view the book not just as a story to be enjoyed (Reading) but as a tool which will provide them with rich pickings in their quest to write a piece of a similar quality (Writing). This is a vital switch in emphasis that should not be underestimated. It gets back to the heart of the debate; namely "What is Guided Reading for?" Maybe the answer is that it is not for reading at all but is instead a crucial stimulus for writing.

The Strategic Role of Shared Reading

In light of the above one might wonder whether Guided Reading in its current form has any place in the Literacy Curriculum. I think it may well do, but it would seem to me that our present practice, which springs out of our own interpretation of Guided Reading, relates more to the practice of "Shared Reading" than pure Guided Reading. The deconstruction of text, at present undertaken in our Guided Reading sessions, would be better served being part of the Literacy lesson. Similarly where the text is read by the teacher with a shared version for all the children to view and follow then the teacher is able to engage the children in higher level of thinking and literary skills because the barrier of decoding the text has been removed. This is where the Guided Reading philosophy can get muddled in its thinking. To many, it was sold as the main source of teaching children to read, after the "hearing each child read" approach was slated by Ofsted (The Teaching of Reading – Ofsted, 1996) and yet all the guidance on Guided Reading points towards the main focus being upon accessing the principles of writing conventions. Certainly in my mind the latter are best served embedded in both the Literacy and the broader curriculum as a whole.

Children's love of Literature

Seemingly unrelated but pertinent to the wider debate are the findings of Guy Claxton *(What is the point of school? Claxton, 2008)* who draws on linear studies to show that one of the major determining factors in a child's ultimate success in life is how much they loved reading when they were of primary school age. So whilst politicians make much of the (supposed) "rising standards in Literacy" as monitored through the SAT scores others see the landscape slightly different. Guy Claxton states that, *"The UK's authoritative Cambridge Review of Primary Education in 2008 found that literacy levels have remained almost static since the 1950s. Over the same period, children's enjoyment of reading — their feel for its pleasures and purposes — has significantly declined." (What is the point of school? Claxton 2008)* The NFER study in 2007 confirmed the same in their report *"Attitudes to reading at ages nine and eleven"* and when comparative studies are made internationally our children fare no better. The following is a quote from *Readers and Reading: the National Report for England 2006. "The data shows that children in England had less positive attitudes to reading than children in most other countries and that their attitudes were somewhat poorer than in 2001. Of particular concern is the 15 per cent of children in the sample for England who had the least positive attitudes, a significant increase from 2001. This is one of the highest proportions in all the participating countries in 2006."* If Guy Claxton's comments relating to this being a predictor of later success are accepted these statistics make frightening reading.

There is a growing consensus amongst many in the academic field that the enjoyment of reading is being undermined by two key factors. One is the constant use of excerpts in literacy lessons without any continuity given to the narrative and the consequent enjoyment of the whole story. To be fair Guided Reading offers a consistency of narrative in this regard through its use of a constant book. However, the other reason proposed by many is the constant unpacking and unpicking of the text which for many destroys the essence of the story, the most enjoyable part of the reading experience.

Does Guided Reading have any place in the Literacy Curriculum?

I believe that it maybe has a strategic role to play but feel it is probably more limited than has previously been thought and to this end it should be used judiciously.

If one takes the Reading strand of the National Curriculum then (leaving aside the breadth of study) the skills in each Key Stage could be summarised as follows;

Key Stage 1 Summary

Reading Strategies
- Learn to Read using phonics, word recognition, grammar and context
- Learn about sentence structure and meaning and develop knowledge of book conventions

Reading for Information
- Be taught the organisational features of non-fiction writing

Literature
- Teach about the different types of texts
- Identify and describe characters, events and settings in fiction
- Sequence and retell stories, predicting events
- Express preferences, giving reasons
- Identify rhyme and sounds in poems, recite and act out stories and poems
- Respond imaginatively in different ways to what they read

Language Structure and Organisation
- Learn about different types of text

Key Stage 2 Summary

Understanding Texts
- Inference and Deduction
- Looking for meaning beyond the literal

Reading for Information
- Distinguish between fact and opinion
- Scan and Skim
- Use a range of text features to obtain meaning
- Consider an argument critically

Literature
- Recognise effect of figurative language, vocabulary and constructing sentences
- Identify how character plot, narrative structure themes and setting are created,
- Recognise the differences between author, narrator and character
- Evaluate ideas, extend thinking and support their views through the text,
- Consider poetic forms and read aloud

Non-fiction texts
- Identify specialist vocabulary and words associated with non-fiction
- Recognise phrases and sentences that convey a formal, impersonal tone
- Identify links between ideas and sentences in non-chronological writing
- Understand the structural and organisational features of different types of text
- Evaluate different formats, layouts and presentational devices
- engage with challenging and demanding subject matter

The first sentence in the KS1 list; *"Learning to Read using phonics, word recognition"* is where the guided reading session should be focused. The guided reading sessions should be used to "teach" children how to read. There is no reason why this should not continue for those on the SEN register later in the school. However beyond the opening sentence the rest of the list should be placed into the Literacy lesson where they can be taught in the context of the broader learning in the class.

So too at Key Stage 2; assuming that the children are now on the "reading to learn" rather than on the "learning to read" continuum I would propose that the sections entitled *"Literature"* and *"Non Fiction texts"* should be taught within the Literacy lesson. *"Reading for Information"* should be tackled through a literacy focused lesson within a foundation subject such as exploring the concept of fact and opinion in a History text. This leaves *"Understanding Texts"* which may need to be taught through Guided Reading sessions of sorts. However at present Guided Reading takes up anywhere between 2-2½ hours a week in most classes nationally and it seems hard to justify allocating this amount of time to just two aspects of the English Curriculum.

So whilst Guided Reading sessions in KS1 may be limited, in the first instance, to areas of "The Teaching of Reading" from Year 2 onwards, Guided Reading should be limited to discussions of the text that are macro in nature and draw on the child's knowledge of the text as a whole. The discussion should operate more under the principles of a "book club" where each member of the group can contribute thoughts and opinions and engage with the text. The teacher takes the role of the "facilitator" as opposed to being the "instructor" and although they may scaffold the discussion towards a focus on inference, deduction and meaning beyond the literal, (elements from the Programmes of Study) the discussion should be of a socio-constructivist nature, where children and teacher "construct" the learning for themselves. This approach reflects the philosophy of

Guided Reading in its purest form, marrying up both the teaching of the textual landscape in a pedagogical framework of "Guided Participation"

Having said that, teachers should be aware that the small group setting of the Guided Reading group is not the only arena where this style of teaching can be undertaken. Whilst it could be argued that the discussion might be richer in a streamed, small group setting, based around a differentiated text, one could also argue the case that any lesson would be better served taught in this style. Sadly in a class of 30 this luxury is not afforded to us. Therefore teachers should use their professional judgement with regards to which lessons warrant such an approach. They need to be pragmatic and judicious with the time they use to target small groups and should weigh up on a lesson by lesson basis whether this approach is justified or whether there are viable alternatives.

Certainly there are two other avenues that teachers could explore when seeking to engage children with texts. The shared reading time in the literacy lesson could have a focus on textual comprehension as it does not have to be used exclusively to deconstruct text as a stepping stone to a child's own written work. Whether the lesson is given over exclusively to this aspect or simply forms part of the learning for that lesson is at the discretion of the teacher. The shared reading option has an advantage over its guided reading counterpart in that the teacher accesses the text for the child allowing them to engage with the comprehension at a potentially higher level.

Another option is for the teacher to read a novel to the class and use this as a stimulus for quality comprehension work. The reading may occur predominantly outside of the literacy lesson in the first instance but again it has the advantage that the teacher reads the text to the child thereby dismantling the "reading barrier" for some children.

Conclusion - Points for Action

In conclusion it would seem to me that Guided Reading will be best taught when each teacher has a secure understanding of what they are trying to achieve in the sessions they classify as "Guided Reading". Learning will only ensue where there is a clear understanding of what areas of Literacy they are seeking to cover within each lesson and how this will be assessed. But above all teachers should have a clear rationale as to why the "Guided Reading small group" scenario is the best arena in which to teach a given concept. They should also be able to articulate clearly why other teaching forums e.g. whole class teaching are not appropriate for the task in question.

Alongside this, where the focus group is considered appropriate, the teacher should heed the evidence from the Ofsted report on reading from 2004. It stated that most of the guided reading sessions... *"took too little account of the needs of other groups in the class and the tasks set for them lacked challenge."* the learning within the "independent" groups should be at least "good" if not "outstanding". This requires that each lesson should ensure that *"the teaching is effective in ensuring that pupils are motivated and engaged and is securing good progress and learning. The work enthuses and challenges most pupils and contributes to good progress. Good and imaginative use is made of resources, including new technology and other adults' support is well focused making a significant contribution to the quality of learning."(Ofsted evaluation schedule for a "Good" lesson)* Where the teacher can discern that the lesson planned will fall below this standard they should use their professional judgement to ascertain how the concept could be taught in a manner where every child makes good progress within the lesson not just the chosen few in the focus group.

THE PROBLEM WITH PROBLEMS

The problem with Problems

Problem Solving has lain at the heart of the Maths Curriculum in Primary schools for many years and indeed the new curriculum 2014 places a greater emphasis on this element. However, it is all too easy to take the bland label of some supposed innovative issue and apply it in such a shallow fashion that it rips the heart out of what was truly intended as an excellent piece of curriculum thinking. I do feel that quality teaching of problem solving has all too often fallen into a deep, dark educational crevasse becoming morphed into something that is so diluted as to become unrecognisable in terms of good classroom practice.

Word Problems or just words?

Many have come to equate problem solving with those written questions found at the end of a given chapter in the Maths textbook. *"Tom has 4 cats and 3 fish. How many pets does he have altogether?"* The expected answer is 7, but this assumes that none of the cats have eaten any of the fish in which case it could be any number between 4 or 7. And here is the issue; problems should be set in the real world, solving (surprisingly enough!), real problems. The clue is in the title, and yet so many word problems are simply a linguistic presentation of a standard algorithm.

As Jo Boaler point out this leads to children developing a context for their Maths learning in an arena she calls "Mathsland". She cites the following example: *A pizza is divided into fifths for friends at a party. Three of the friends eat their slices but then four more friends arrive. What fraction should the following slices be divided into?* No doubt there will be a technically correct numerically based answer in the teacher's handbook that the teacher might use to mark the work in the evening. However, surely in the real world the answers are more likely to be those Jo Boaler offers namely that *"if extra people turn up at a party more pieces are ordered or people go without slices"* She concludes that *"Over time children realise that when you enter "Mathsland" you leave your common sense at the door"*

The truth is that not all problems based on algorithms translated into words have meaning when solved mathematically. As Mike Askew points out the question; *"If Henry VIII had 6 wives then how many did Henry IV have?"* implies that he had 3 but this is another number problem with a one-way ticket to Mathsland.

So bearing in mind that most of these problems lack all sense of reasons and reality what do children need to learn to successfully solve word problems in a classroom context? Well, the first key skill is to realise what Ofsted noted that "Standard problems tend to be associated with exercises at the end of chapters, where pupils know the operation to use is, say, multiplication because the chapter was all about multiplication". (Recent Research in Mathematics Education 5-16, Ofsted) The second survival strategy in the modern Maths classroom is to work out the likely operation from the context of the numbers. Mike Askew tells how he has a Chinese textbook which is written solely in Mandarin apart from the numbers, and whilst he does not read one word of mandarin he writes "I am confident that the problem involving 25 and 14 is most likely to be multiplication while the one with 3007 and 1896 is almost certainly subtraction."

Teaching in such contexts leads to a bland form of numerical understanding that sells children woefully short of the richness that number and Mathematics can offer. Ramya Vivekanandan, UNESCO Education director, analysed the PISA results for Maths in 2012. He showed that those children who relied purely or significantly on memorisation of formulaic strategies to solve calculations were consistently amongst the low achievers, whereas those students who focused on a breadth of Mathematics and developed the "Big Ideas" concepts were the high achievers. Jo Boaler in a lecture at Oxford University (18th December 2014) pointed out that the UK lay 64th out of the 65 countries for having the largest percentage of "memorisers". Only Ireland scored lower. There was a consensus amongst the delegates that it is the UK's obsession with testing that allows children to thrive on such bland, shallow word based material because it is that style of questioning that forms the basis of the tests at the end of Key Stage 2.

So if it is true that many word problems are simply, as Mike Askew points out *"calculations wrapped up in words"* what is problem solving all about and does it, or should it, have such a prominent place in the Maths curriculum?

What is Maths all about anyway?

As with most issues related to education it increasingly seems to me that the key is to stand as far back from the issue as you can to allow the fullest perspective. Then when the macro elements are resolved in the mind, one can drill down to the micro elements of what makes up a scheme of work, a weekly plan, a daily lesson through to the progress of individual children. Because our profession hinges around the classroom and its practice there is always the danger that teachers start with the question: What should I teach tomorrow? But this is flawed if one has not engaged with the deeper and broader questions in the first instance.

So what is "real mathematics?" Volumes have been written on the theme too numerous to replicate here but here is a selection of thoughts. Galileo stated that *"Mathematics is the language with which God wrote the universe"* – not bad for starters! Oswald Veblen, a mathematician living in the last century said *"Mathematics is one of the essential emanations of the human spirit, a thing to be valued in and for itself, like art or poetry."* To these men Maths was so much more than a few calculations undertaken in the lesson before break on a daily basis, to them Maths was a language to live by and a means of making sense of the world.

It is often hard to recognise our "calculation-dominated" curriculum with either of the comments above but to be fair the Programmes of Study for the previous National Curriculum held philosophical statements for the teaching of each subject and calculation was not a major focus (indeed it was not even mentioned) in its rationale. It said: *"Mathematics equips pupils with a uniquely powerful set of tools to understand and change the world. These tools include logical reasoning, problem-solving skills, and the ability to think in abstract ways."* It went on to include the following quote from Professor Ruth Lawrence, University of Michigan *"Maths is the study of patterns abstracted from the world around us – so anything we learn in maths has literally thousands of applications, in arts, sciences, finance, health and leisure!"*

Recently I watched the film *"Enigma"*, a story about the codebreakers in the war based at Bletchley. Those seeking to decipher the codes were all mathematicians. At one point in the film one of the girls turns to Tom Jericho and asks him; *"Why are you a mathematician? Do you like sums?"* Tom replies *"No, I like numbers, because with numbers, truth and beauty are the same thing. You know you're getting somewhere when the equations start looking beautiful"*

To those well versed in the subject, Mathematics is not primarily about calculation. Calculators calculate and we carry these in pencil cases or access them on our mobile phones. Mathematicians are those who see the big picture, the patterns and relationships in numbers and how these relate to situations and problems in their world.

Conrad Wolfham is a mathematician and the head of Wolfram Alpha, a company that seeks to develop IT applications. His TED talk has had over 1 million hits and is entitled *"Teaching Kids Real Maths"* It seeks to establish a clear rationale for the teaching of the subject. His premise is that any Maths problem is founded on four stages:

1. Posing the right questions *(The key to finding any solution is to ask the right question)*
2. Real World to Maths Computation *(Taking a problem and turning it into a Maths based problem for analysis)*
3. Computation *(Crunching the numbers)*
4. Maths formulation real world verification *(Putting the solution back into the real world for verification)*

He maintains that schools are focusing their energies on the wrong elements within these four. *"Here is the crazy thing"* he says *"in Maths education we are spending about 80% of the time teaching people to do step 3 by hand but this is the one step that computers can do better than any human... instead we ought to be getting students to focus on the conceptualising of problems and applying them and getting the teacher to run through with them how to do that."* I would contend that there is more than an element of truth in what he advocates. We live in the throes of a technological revolution that is transforming the world and transmuting every aspect of society. This new dawn is one based on logical thinking and reasoning more than any other skill and Maths is the native language of that digital world.

Problem Solving set in this context

In light of the above we need to be developing a fresh form of Maths that engages children on a totally different level. It is tragic to think that one girl said of her Maths lessons *"In maths you just have to remember but in other subjects you think about it"* (quoted by Jo Boaler in her book *"The elephant in the classroom"*). The truth is that much of our Maths curriculum is "calculation focused" preventing children embracing the true Maths that those more conversant with the subject readily recognise.

Quality problem solving resolves this tension. It has at its heart the observation of patterns. It develops persistence and risk taking alongside logical thinking processes that encourage children to tackle tasks systematically. They also develop the ability to recognise numerical relationships in their initial findings. Jane Jones is the Chief HMI for Maths and in the "Ofsted Better Maths" series of conferences she stated that *"The degree of emphasis on problem solving (and conceptual understanding) is a key discriminator between good and weaker provision"*. This may well simply be due to the fact that it is these schools that have engaged most with the Maths teaching rationale and therefore are generally more cogent in their planning but whatever the reason good problem solving lies at the heart of good Maths teaching. It is interesting to note that none of this is a new message; the Cockcroft report published in 1982 described *"problem solving as lying at the 'heart' of mathematics"*

The National Primary Strategy produced a document in 2004 in which they outlined the five types of problem solving:
- Finding all possibilities;
- Logic problems;
- Finding rules and describing patterns;
- Diagram problems and visual puzzles;
- Word problems.

For reasons I have articulated above I would raise an objection to the inclusion of "word problems" and would place it back into the calculation section of the curriculum where I believe it truly belongs, but that aside the above offers a good starting point for a framework.

From here teachers need to source problems, either within the context of real world scenarios or from sources which deliver the type of Mathematician that we need to secure for the 21st Century. Without wishing to labour the obvious the quality of learning will be dictated by the quality of the problem the teacher sets for the children. But if we continue to focus on the attributes we wish to develop through these activities which are; resilience, risk taking, creativity, posing questions, exploring through trial and error and developing a systematic approach it should be self-evident which activities will most effectively deliver these. As most teachers are aware the DfE Primary Strategy materials and the NRich website are rich sources of quality material, as is the newly created SPEAR Maths which seeks to present not just problems in themselves but also a framework to work within.

Teaching Problems

One of the points the Primary Strategy made to good effect in its document is that teaching needs to reflect the outcomes from the task. It states that, *"Children need to be taught the strategies and to be shown how they can apply these systematically to problem solving. For many children the hit-and-miss approach they use when gathering information and their poor management of information limits their ability to work systematically." (Problem Solving Primary Strategy 2004)* Therefore teaching should focus on either creating and extending the open ended nature of the task or developing cogent strategies for children to solve such problems.

Jane Jones showed the following problem (on following page) to delegates at a recent conference. The problem is not complex in and of itself but she was encouraging teachers to focus on the strategies they used to solve the puzzle. The likelihood is that you spotted that the 3 cows in the middle row must be multiples of 3 that total 15. From this point the puzzle starts to unlock. We should not assume that children will necessarily see this without a secure amount of scaffolding to support them. The lesson therefore needs to focus on the development of the systematic skills required rather than leaving children with the impression that the key feature is "finding out the value of the pig"

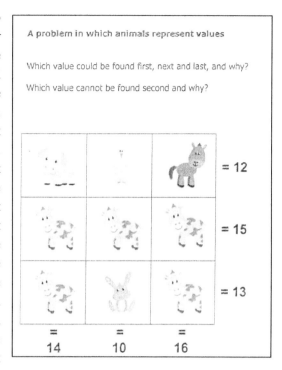

A problem in which animals represent values

Which value could be found first, next and last, and why?

Which value cannot be found second and why?

All too often it is easy for teachers to lose sight of what the problem solving lesson is for and it thus reverts subliminally into a calculation style of lesson where the primary focus can become "finding the answer" But just as good calculation lessons should focus on the process and explore the most "effective and efficient" method (wording of the Numeracy Strategy), so the teaching of problems should not focus solely on the answer but on the mathematical skills and processes the children are gaining along the way. It is essential that children build on these throughout the Maths curriculum.

Alan Schoenfeld makes an interesting observation related to this when he says that whilst the idea of *problems* has always been a key element in the maths curriculum, *problem solving* has not. What he is seeking to clarify is that children need to develop a "toolkit" of "problem solving" strategies rather than accessing a series of answers and solutions to an eclectic group of problems unrelated in any form to each other. The Primary Strategy document sought to emphasise this with its advice regarding medium term planning. It suggested *"Over a week, the children learn how to apply the strategies they have been taught in a particular lesson to similar problems in the following lessons."* There is more than an element of wisdom in this approach.

There are of course a range of strategies that children should acquire under the umbrella of Maths Problem Solving. This might include:
- Trial and improvement – to be introduced as a valid starting point
- Working systematically – finding all possibilities within a problem
- Working logically – maintaining inputs whilst changing variables
- Pattern Recognition – looking for rules and patterns within numbers, shape patterns etc.

Teaching Maths in this way treats the subject as an inter-connected discipline that from time immemorial has provided solutions to some of history's most intriguing problems. It is essential to everyday life, critical to science, technology and engineering, and necessary for financial literacy and most forms of employment. A high-quality mathematics education therefore provides a foundation for understanding the world, the ability to reason mathematically, an appreciation of the beauty and power of mathematics and a sense of enjoyment and curiosity about the subject.

Without wishing to labour the point the word "calculation" does not feature within the last paragraph. This is not to say that calculation is not important, as we all know, it is the foundational building block within a child's mathematical development but it must not remain the sole raison d'etre for the primary curriculum. This would be to sell children, and indeed the subject of Maths itself, woefully short.

THE SHALLOW STRATEGY OF "COUNTING ON"

The Difference between Counting on and Calculation

The distinction between "counting on" and addition is clear. The latter is a calculation strategy whereas counting relates to one to one correspondence and a basic understanding of the number system relating to place value. Whilst these are crucial building blocks in the early learning of mathematics they can be stumbling blocks to the acquisition of calculation skills later if they are not taught in an appropriate context at an early age. I am sure it is possible to add 287 to 134 by counting on, but I doubt if it would be described by anyone as "efficient and effective" (the wording of the Numeracy Strategy) The reality is that children need to move beyond simple counting if they are to become proficient in calculation.

So whilst few would argue that *"counting should constitute the basis of the early years number curriculum" (Development of Numeracy Concepts, Nunes 2001)* we need to recognise that a overly prolonged exposure to "counting on" as a sole strategy may hinder a child's ability to move fluently into calculation.

Breaking down the Counting Culture

There is a danger that some of the strategies we use to teach children early number concepts may well actually embed the wrong approach into their mathematical psyche and thus have the potential to undermine the bigger picture of creating fluent mathematicians in the longer term.

Thompson *(Teaching and Learning Early Number, 1997)* has produced a classification of number strategies and their relation to counting. These include counting up and down, doubling, bridging up and down, step counting and regrouping. Seen in this context the concept of "counting" in the Early Years takes on a broader dimension. So whilst it is totally appropriate for children to use "counting on" in the first instance this should be used as a springboard to build in more concrete calculation strategies.

Bridging is a key building block in the calculation process. So when adding 8+4 we might be happy for the child to add 8+1+1+1+1 in the first instance but we would want them to refine this approach at some point so that they added 8+1+1 and to understand they had reached a ten and appreciate the significance of this. They should then be encouraged to reflect on whether the 2 they have needs to be "counted on" or whether they can in fact simply "calculate" the answer by adding the remaining 2 onto the 10. Not only is this accessing number for the child but it is also building within the child a secure foundation in terms of later calculation strategies they will need to adopt where the concept of bridging becomes a key building block in the process. This dovetails into the need for children to understand the concept and the power of "known-facts" (as the Numeracy Strategy called them) for as children become conversant in number bonds the need for any counting is thus removed. As Penny Munn points out Thompson's work *"shows how number knowledge is based on a network of strategies that include both counting and conceptual advances on counting."(Teaching and learning numeracy in the early years, 2001)*

The key is that the children are quickly moved on from solely counting as a central strategy as soon as is conceptually possible for them as learners. Research clearly demonstrates that *"children who don't move on from counting are disadvantaged and require intervention; such ideas form the basis of early years mental maths. (Munn, 2001)* Gray underscores this as he states that *"counting has a positive role early in development, but needs to be replaced quite rapidly by more sophisticated cognitive concepts."* *(Compressing the Counting Process, 1997)* This creates an additional issue *"that an over-dependence on counting may lead to their not committing number facts to memory" (Nunes 2001)* this will seriously impair their ability to make effective progress in terms of true mathematical calculation.

The key role of Bridging in Calculation

The bridging process is key in the teaching of calculation. As stated above the children should be actively discouraged from adding 18+8 using 18+1+1+1 and encouraged to see that adding 2 will take them to 20. The children in KS1 may resist this because with smaller numbers they may still claim the "counting on" method is fit for purpose in this context. Whilst this may be true in the short term, the lack of ability to be dexterous with number bonds will find them sadly wanting in the more demanding environment of Key Stage 2 where numbers increase markedly.

If we are to develop a secure foundation in calculation throughout the school then the following strategies should be used:

(i) The Number Line
The number line is predominantly a calculation tool and should therefore only be used as such. The number line even into Key Stage 3 is described as *"informal pencil and paper notes, recording some or all of the solution, becoming part of a mental strategy"* it advocates the number line as one way of *"acquiring a repertoire of mental calculation strategies" (NNS*

Framework for Year 7 p6) It therefore needs to be used judiciously where it is functioning as a means of developing foundational mathematical understanding.

If the following strategy is used to calculate on a number line there is the real danger that it is simply driving home to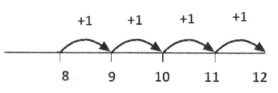
children that the essential strategy required in a calculation is the need to "count on" This is especially detrimental in this example as the method one would be hoping to instil in the child at this juncture would be the process of "bridging" and the use of known facts derived through their number bonds.

(ii) The use of Dienes Material
The use of Dienes material must also be thought through when used in the context of calculation. The Dienes materials provide a rich visual picture of numbers so many classes will rightly use them to demonstrate place value and the relationship between tens and units. Such that two tens and 5 units is 25 (as demonstrated right).

However when used to add 25 to 15 as in the example below there is the potential for the separate units to herald to the child that the most

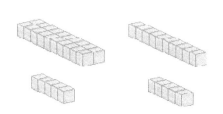
appropriate strategy is to "count on" using the cubes as individual units (see picture on the next page). Whilst there is no-one who would not advocate the use of materials in the teaching of Maths concepts at this stage in a child's development,

 the tragedy is that the apparatus may well be driving the Maths down the "Counting" route rather than leading children towards the bridging principle which they will require to make effective progress in calculation.

Akin to this is another related issue. If this approach does not lead the child down the route of "counting on" then the Dienes material certainly fosters and effectively models the approach of the more formal calculations found in standard written calculations. Whereas traditional algorithms treat 56 as 5 tens and 6 units, thereby necessitating understanding of the column value aspect of each digit, mental calculations rely more on what has been called the "quantity value aspect of place value" where 56 is seen by the child as 50 and 6. Since the numeracy strategy does not recommend the teaching of column addition until Year 4 there would appear to be little need to embark on the more complex mathematical concept of an individual digit being allocated a value on the basis of its column value before the child has fully appreciated and used numbers fully in mental calculation strategies.

Indeed there is also an argument to be made that 50 makes more "number sense" to a child than the more abstract "5 in a tens column" The desire for children to gain an early understanding of column value is a relic from the days when the column algorithm was the end goal and therefore the understanding of place value was a key staging post on the journey towards this final destination. In the rich and broader world of mental calculation there are many other avenues to explore and therefore the use of Dienes and other related material should be used judiciously and wisely.

In terms of the "counting on" debate if we wish to use apparatus to enhance the children's understanding then it may be that products such as Numicon or Cuisinaire rods have a greater power in demonstrating the correct calculation principles to children.

Numicon allows the child to add 7+3 but also allows the child to see the process as two distinct numbers in their own right. I have no doubt that the child may well add 7+ 1+1+1 at this point but they are still gaining the understanding that even though they are "counting on" there are two numbers being added, and this is accentuated visually. This alongside a  programme of number bond teaching will allow the child to appreciate that this calculation should hinge on the use of number bonds and addition, rather than simply counting on

This can be built on later when they come to learn bridging. The principles remain the same except now the addition of 7+7 can be demonstrated through the creating of a number bond to 10 and then by adding on 4. This drives home the concept of addition as opposed to "counting on". Again I can accept that many children may well "count on" the two sets of numbers and bypass the bridging process in the first instance but using this method they are permanently reminded through the use of a very powerful visual tool that there is a more  *"efficient and effective"* (NNS wording again) if they use their number bonds. These subliminal messages are very powerful at this stage in the child's development.

The same power to drive calculation towards addition is afforded by the Cuisinaire rods, which, whilst seemingly similar to the Dienes material

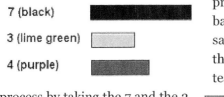

7 (black)

3 (lime green)

4 (purple)

provide a completely different concept base when it comes to calculation. The same calculation can be done using the following rods and should the teacher wish they can underscore the

process by taking the 7 and the 3 and making a 10 of them as illustrated on the right.

10 (orange)

4 (purple)

Both these last two methods drive the child away from "counting on" and more towards a stage where they can see a deeper appreciation of the role of number bonds in the calculation phase.

Known Facts are the tools of Creative Mathematics

It is therefore self-evident that the use of known facts is a key transition phase as the children move from a stage of understanding the number system and how the principles of addition work into an arena where they calculate fluently and effectively. Whilst the child may have to learn their number bonds and times tables by rote and may lack a full appreciation of their understanding; these "known facts" are the gateway to learning effectively in the area of creative Mathematics. When undertaking higher ordered mathematical tasks children should be solely focused on *"choosing the appropriate operation and method of calculation" (NNS p82-3)* Where instant recall is lacking they often struggle to fulfil the task because they are engaged in two parallel tasks; namely selecting the correct calculation method as well as developing strategies to solve that same calculation. In the sense that the former is a higher order skill, the children who lack secure knowledge of "known facts" struggle to fulfil such tasks.

Learning without Understanding

Whilst it seems a little incongruous to learn these facts without a full understanding of their mathematical meaning, the rote aspect of the learning must be seen as a process not as an end goal. As has been said you cannot be creative unless you have the tools with which to be creative (Arthur Cropley's work on creativity) Therefore the purpose of the rote learning is to put these mathematical tools into the hands of children so they can explore the underlying understanding as they use them in a range of contexts.

Known and Derived Facts

The rote learning should be restricted to the number bonds to 10 (addition only) in the first instance as these are the key elements needed in the teaching of bridging. The number bonds should then be increased to 20 to learn facts such as 8+4 that bridge 10 and then the times table up to 10x10 (multiplication only). The goal of seeking "instant recall" in facts beyond these has the potential to stunt the ability of children to explore and develop "derived facts". Research shows that *"those who can make links between known and deduced facts make good progress, because the known and the derived support each other." (M. Askew: "They're counting on us" June 2008)* In this sense..."*these two aspects of mental mathematics – known facts and derived facts – are complimentary. Higher attaining pupils are able to use known facts to figure out other number facts." (Gray EM 1991).* The reality is that if children develop an over-reliance on rote learning they lose the skill of fluently using derived facts and tend instead, to resort to a default mechanism which is often "counting on". As Askew points out; *"This is one of the reasons that the national Numeracy strategy initially advocated delaying the introduction of standard algorithms. The danger is that children can appear to be confident in working with large numbers but they are actually only dealing with single digits and using counting on procedures".*

On the basis of this understanding the school holds that:

1. All rote learning should be limited to the number bonds to 10 and times table up to 10x10. Children do not need to "know" what 12x12 is but instead they should be encouraged to use cogent strategies to derive the answer from known facts. Eventually these "derived" facts may well become "known" facts but this needs to come out of a correct philosophical understanding that seeks to take children deeper in their understanding of how numbers relate to one another in a range of calculations. The truth is that as a *"child's range of known number facts expands, the range of strategies available for deriving new facts expands as well" (M. Askew June 2008)* However this richness of mathematical understanding does not occur if the process is bypassed through rote learning.

2. The "instant recall" does exactly what it says on the tin. When gauging whether children have "instant recall" teachers should work on the basis that a child should be able to answer times tables questions at a rate of one every 2 seconds in a test situation. Any speed less than this would tend to imply that the children are "calculating" the answers and they should be pushed towards an instant recall of these facts.

The Power of Mental Calculation over Counting on

The truth is that our ultimate goal should not just be that children can calculate using pen and paper if the numbers are set out in columns but instead we should be training children to see patterns and relationships in numerical calculations such that they become mentally dexterous in their mathematical thinking. It has long been recognised that the higher attaining pupils are not those that can turn out pages and pages of correct sums but are those who can relate Maths to real contexts and can "see" their way through calculations by using a wide range of mental strategies. The child who seeks to calculate 234+199 using the standard column algorithm has been fed a very narrow and deficient mathematical diet. The first question one should ask when faced with any calculation should be *Can I do this in my head?* In fairness the original Numeracy Document produced in 1998 had this as a central focus and drove mental calculation hard both through the use of the "Mental and Oral Starter" as well as through the framework as a whole. It is true that government research has shown that children since the introduction of the framework were often overloaded with strategies and I would agree that the balance needs to be addressed. However one of the tragedies of the renewed framework is that we have moved away from the core focus of mental calculation and this is to the detriment of good Maths teaching.

It is interesting to note how many of the 2-digit by 2-digit calculations (which are the key feature of the KS2 curriculum) we might expect children to complete mentally. If we take addition for example and take all the numbers between 1 and 100 there are 9,900 combinations of sums that can be made. If you now take the mental calculations from the original Numeracy framework and set these against them we find that there are only a relative few where you might expect children to resort to a strategy other than a mental calculation.

Mental Calculation Strategy	Using mental method
All the numbers with a ten e.g. 10 +7 or 50 +16	**1890**
Any calculation with a 1 in the units because 42+21 allows partitioning and/or where the number is 39 the addition of 1 unit does not require bridging	**1890**
Any number that has a 9 in the units should be easily added using the "Add 10 and subtract 1" method	**1890**

All the numbers which have a number bond to 10 in the units should be added using the known fact of the number bond to 10 e.g. 37+13	**1000**
Where no bridging is involved then partitioning should be able to be done mentally e.g. 13+14	**4500**
Any number where the units contain a double should be mentally added e.g. 42+32	**900**
Any numbers which use "near doubles" could be mentally calculated e.g. 15+16	**900**

Using this analysis it is clear that the majority of the sums require a mental calculation strategy if they are to be solved effectively. For example nearly half the sums require no bridging and therefore a simple partitioning of the tens and the units should suffice as an efficient and effective strategy. Indeed an overwhelming percentage, (88% overall) require a mental calculation approach rather than a pen and paper method.

(NB: For those who have noted that the numbers of the sums do not equate to the total of 9,900 it should be borne in mind that many are subject to "double counting". For example 3+4 is both a "near double" and a total that does not bridge 10)

If one takes all the sums which fall outside the criteria outlined in the Numeracy Framework for mental calculation then they are the calculations where the unit values are as follows:

3+8, 4+7, 4+8, 5+7, 5+8, 6+8, 7+4, 7+5, 8+3, 8+4, 8+5, 8+6

This (along with their reversals e.g. 8+3 etc.) accounts for 1200 of the total of 9,900 which is only 12% of all the calculations available. When one looks at it in these statistical terms it should cause us to reflect on the balance of our teaching. Is 88% of our time spent on mental calculation strategies or on more standard pen and paper methods? There needs to be a redressing of this imbalance so that children become more mentally agile.

To this end it is vital that the children not only move away from "counting on" but are encouraged from a very early age to work towards the richest of mathematical destinations. In the past this was deemed to be the standard algorithm, the perceived panacea of previous generations but true numerical dexterity is gained through the ability to see patterns and relationships in numbers. These are the true foundations on which children can build the capacity to calculate mentally in a wide range of contexts.

Taught or Caught?

Can this be taught or is this just the domain of the higher attaining child in each class? In 2001 Kings College, London undertook a key study entitled *"Raising attainment in primary number sense: from counting to strategy".* They looked at the whole issue of children's lack of effective strategies and in experiments with control groups sought to "teach" children the connections and relationships between numbers that facilitate more effective calculation. Their conclusion was that *"through carefully targeted teaching, pupils who have not developed these strategies for themselves can indeed learn them."* There is encouragement then for schools to continue to move children away from superficial algorithms and into the enriching world of mathematical understanding.

Concluding Remarks

The school should be diligent in bridging the gap between known and derived facts for children, gradually weaning them away from "counting on" at the earliest opportunity. Children should be actively encouraged to see the connection between known facts and derived facts and not treat each calculation as if coming to a blank canvas. The truth is many children see their times tables as the end goal not as the tools that enable them to solve more complex calculations. So children should be shown that to know 3 x 3 = 9 also provides a solution to 30 x 3, and 30 x 30. Similarly children faced with a problem such as 100 ÷ 25 will, all too often, begin by looking for a procedure rather than seeking to establish whether there is a relationship between the numbers as a starting point. This default position needs to be constantly challenged as it is only as children build on their ability to see patterns in number that they will truly develop a rich mathematical understanding.

THE PARTITIONING PREDICAMENT

The inescapable use of partitioning and its associated dangers

Partitioning is fundamental to calculation in primary school. Whilst in the early years children develop calculation based on "knowing and recalling" number facts, as they move into Key stage 2 the numbers become of a size where, recall is incongruous. No child (nor adult for that matter) would "recall" or "know" 2374 + 4736. The numbers need to be broken down so as they can be brought back into the arena where the key question; *"Can I do this in my head?"* can come into play. Thus partitioning is fundamental to primary school mathematics.

However... there are inherent dangers when this approach becomes the core element of the Maths curriculum.
1. It allows all sums to be reduced to a series of single calculations based on number bonds to 10. Whilst this has great power in allowing children to access a mental approach it creates a strategy base that is detrimental to holistic mathematical understanding.
2. It prevents children developing a true "feel for number" in terms of their size, properties and relationships within the number system. This is because children see 324 + 245 as a 3 part calculation involving 3+2; 2+4 and 4+5. This leaves opportunity for them to develop little appreciation for the place value of number.

3. At its worse partitioning allows children to wander through the labyrinth of Mathematical learning without the need to engage with "real" numbers and secure calculations. Children can leave Key Stage 2 with a shallow understanding of calculation that has reduced all sums to a series of unrelated tens and units calculations that sometimes are straightforward e.g. 242+121 and at other times involve little tricks; e.g. "carrying one into the next column" (246+186) and "borrowing one" (214-189). The "little tricks" are viewed by children as irritating hurdles to get over as they continue on their narrow "number bonds to 10" journey. Whereas in truth the "trick" allows them to bypass a major block of mathematical understanding with which they should engage.

4. As one Year 5 girl given the sum 253,254,246 + 132,432,732 noted upon observing that none of the numbers caused issues of "carrying"; "... there is no Maths in that calculation at all it is just a set of simple sums". By the same token the children in the same lesson that calculated 467+288 as 61,415 showed that although they could reduce the sum to a series of simplistic calculations, their associated knowledge of place value was woefully lacking.

Related International Research

i. Recent research from Holland shows clearly that children have a natural propensity to revert to partitioning as a strategy. The reasons for this are not given but I would have thought they were fairly obvious even to the most casual observer in that the children are seeking to simplify complex calculations into an arena where the answer can come within the range of known facts" (Thompson,1999b)

ii. Scrutiny of calculations that rely primarily on partitioning suggests that there is *"no evidence of what is normally understood by place value in their methods"* (Ruthven, 1998).

iii. This is especially true where the column method is adopted. When children are encouraged to use mental calculations their "strategies use what has been described as the quantity value aspect of place value: 56

seen as 50 and 6, whereas standard written algorithms draw on the column aspect: 56 seen as 5 tens and 6 units (Thompson,1999a)

Common Misconceptions in calculation

The lack of understanding is evidenced clearly through the "standard" mistakes children make in their calculations. These provide a window into the mathematical areas of misunderstanding that exist in the mind of the child. These need to be addressed not just as individual conceptual errors, but to look at the deeper mathematical principles that lie behind them so that these may be backfilled as well. For instance issues of place value may relate to simple column confusion but more probably will be an indication that the children see little relationship between numbers in base 10. They may not have a "feel" for how big 1000 is, nor how it fits in the greater number system. It behoves us therefore whenever we enter a calculation lesson to ensure that the method taught seeks to underpin these foundation concepts as well as sharing with the children a particular strategy for a given calculation.

Misconceptions in Four Rules Calculations

Addition

a) Place Value (column method)

$$234$$
$$+216$$
$$540$$
$$1$$

$$24$$
$$+16$$
$$310$$

b) Place Value (non column based) $3.2 + 17 = 49$ or 4.9

c) Relationship of Number $16 + 10 = 25$

d) Relationship within calculations

$$30 + 20 = 50$$
$$\text{therefore...} \quad 50 - 20 = x$$

Subtraction

a) Place Value (Decomposition)

```
  2 5 4        1 5 14
- 1 3 7        1 3  7
               _____
                 2  7
```

b) Number

$$456 - 264 = 400 - 200 = 200$$
$$50 - 60 = 10$$
$$6 - 4 = 2$$

c) Relationship of Number

$$87 - 20 = 66$$

d) Relation of Calculation

$$50 - 20 = 30$$
$$\text{therefore...} \quad 30 + 20 = x$$

Multiplication

a) Computational Understanding

$$24 \times 12 = \quad 20 \times 10 = 200$$
$$4 \times 2 = \underline{\quad 8}$$
$$208$$

b) Place value/ Computational Understanding

$$145 \times 30 = 145{,}000$$

c) Place value

$$\begin{array}{r} 2\ 4 \\ \underline{\times\ 1\ 2} \\ 8 \\ 4\ 0 \\ 4\ 0 \\ \underline{2\ 0} \\ \underline{1\ 0\ 8} \end{array}$$

Division

a) Place Value/Feel for Number $242 \div 12$

$$242 \div 10 =\ 24.2$$
$$242 \div\ \ 2 =\ \underline{85.5}$$
$$=\underline{109.7}$$

b) Place Value

$$600 \div 30 = 2$$

c) Computational Understanding

$$540 \div 20 = 52$$

d) Relationship within calculations

therefore...

$$3 \times 5 = 15$$
$$5 \div 15 = 3$$

Estimation within calculation

Alongside all these calculation errors is the fact that many children in the upper reaches of Key Stage 2 have traditionally struggled with attaining a reasonable estimation for a calculation and often produced answers that showed a complete lack of understanding for the "feel for the numbers".

These two examples are from a more able group of Year 6 children
a)   427 x 27 = 149,286
b)   376 x 26 =   64,523

Within the same group of children were some who struggled to give accurate estimates for calculations such as 36 x 27 when this was set as an isolated task. They all struggled to estimate answers that contained decimals.

Why do children keep returning to the partitioning method?

When we asked our own children here at the school as to why they returned to the partitioning method there were not real surprises in the reasons given. Primarily they used partitioning to make complex calculations appear more accessible. The following are comments from Year 6 children:
 "When you split it up the numbers look quite nice and small"
"You can make them into small sums and they look easy"

There may be little we can do about this for as international research shows *"children have a natural propensity to revert to partitioning"* (Thompson)

However the second reason is more pertinent to our deliberations in that the methods we present to children, especially in the first instance, have a profound impact on their later preferred method
"Partitioning was the first method we were taught so we keep returning to it" (Year 6 child)

Whilst it is clear that children gain much success from the use of the number line, recent *research "indicates that after some initial success in using the model to develop mental methods, most children reverted to formal methods within two months. This may change if its introduction precedes formal methods"* (Rousham, 1997)

What the research shows is that the first form of calculation introduced to children has a powerful impact on their later development. This means it is vital that consideration is given to the order in which methods are introduced, and that this is embedded in a clear framework of progression at a whole school level.

Key Features of a Whole School Calculation Policy

In the light of the above I would suggest that the two key factors that need to be addressed are:
i)   The children's lack of feel for number
ii)   The lack of true mathematical understanding of what is occurring within the process of a given calculation

I would therefore propose the following to address these:

i. The method we teach children is the one outlined in the school's Calculation Document (available at www.wyche.worcs.sch.uk) This has a heavy focus on what our Year 5 children came to call "Half Partitioning"; where one of the numbers in any calculation remains as a whole and only the subsequent numbers are partitioned. i.e. 245 + 352 = becomes 245 + 300 + 50 + 2 as opposed to a series of partitioned calculations focusing on the single digits of 2+3, 4+5 and 5+2
   This allows children to focus on the *"quantity value aspect of place value"* where 56 is seen as 50 and 6. (Thompson 1999a)

ii. To facilitate this more effectively the use of the number line should become the primary tool for calculation. It is both visible and, in conjunction with the approach outlined above, allows children to engage with the "real" numbers as opposed to a set of single digit calculations out of context.

iii. The children should be presented with the number line as a base model and, more importantly, as the first model that they encounter when tackling new calculations. As we have seen the initial introduction of any calculation method is one of the greatest determining factors in its future use by children.

iv. The use of the column method should not be introduced until the latter stages of KS2. By this time children will have a secure understanding of the operations of the four rules. I fear that earlier introduction of these methods adds little to mathematical understanding and has the potential to be used by children as a route to bypass true mathematical cognition. Its introduction should be seen as simply an additional strategy for children to use when appropriate rather the definitive, all-encompassing strategy to be used for all calculations.
"Children tend to use algorithms as mechanical and where they do not understand the procedures the research evidence suggests that they are unable to reconstruct the processes involved" (Anghileri 2001)

v. The school should regularly undertake a thorough review of its Maths resources. If we feel that children are losing a "feel for number" then the use of these concrete materials to model concepts may become a key feature in addressing this. Whilst Piaget informs us that in the pre-operational stage (ages 2-7) the child cannot conceptualise abstractly, it would appear that our children, in the supposed "concrete" phase (ages 7-11), would similarly benefit from such support. Deines blocks, the decimal and fractions blocks etc. were all once standard fare in classrooms but current teaching would appear to have become a little more abstract. Certainly those children in the lower end of the academic spectrum at KS2 who, by definition, will be pre-operational would benefit greatly for a more kinaesthetically based approach.

Will this not lead to didactic teaching?

Not at all; the key is that in allowing children to explore and play around with numbers we will be "scaffolding" them towards a given solution that we know will enhance understanding.

To illustrate, here are a series of lessons taught to Year 4/5 children on subtraction:

- In the opening lesson the children were presented with a calculation such as 246 -158.
- Initial solutions offered by the children contained a series of errors including the classical 40–50=10, others partitioned and added the resultant calculation as opposed to subtracting from the original number.
- The strategies were logged on the board. They were then analysed for their effectiveness. The majority had chosen a partitioned method and could readily see the downfalls within it once the calculations were discussed
- The teacher then suggested a method that incorporated their desire to partition with a means of alleviating the issues that partitioning both numbers created.
- The children bought into it because it made "connections" with issues they had encountered for themselves. It is this "buying in" process which lies at the heart of the emergent approach. The key is that children seek their own solutions to their own problems but can readily see the shortcomings in them when a more efficient method is modelled by a peer or by the teacher,
- The children consolidated the strategy over the next few lessons

What about SEN children... Should they not be taught the "easier", more accessible column method?

The construct lying behind such a question as this is the notion that whilst the number line may well be a purer way of teaching the concept of number, for some children many feel it would be easier to resort to column addition. Thereby children simply need to know their number bonds to 10 to complete the task because the 4 and the 2 in 456+278 can be seen as 4+2=6 without any real knowledge of place value. The argument goes that if some children struggle to bypass understanding this provides a ready-made solution they could use to survive.

Surely Maths teaching should be richer than providing children with a catalogue of tricks to bypass true understanding? However, even if we park the debate on whether teaching should remain aspirational in terms of pedagogical philosophy or become more pragmatic responding to the ability and the needs of the child, research by Gray and Tall offers a useful insight.

They gave a number of children across a wide ability range a selection of addition and subtraction sums to do. Their conclusions were fascinating. The above average children in Year 4 used the "counting on" strategy only 9% of the time to solve the calculations given. However those children who were deemed below average by their teacher used this strategy 72% of the time. When the curriculum given to the children was carefully studied it was found that the less able children were being taught a completely different Maths syllabus to their peers and as Jo Boaler concludes *"the Maths that the low achievers are learning is a more difficult subject" (The Elephant in the Room p139)* She draws on the example of the complexity found in counting back in the sum 16-13. The method is slow, cumbersome and *"the room for mistakes is huge" (p140)* The research showed clearly that as the children moved through the school they became increasingly disadvantaged by the paucity of their understanding in the subject. The reality is that Maths is a linear subject in that any new concept builds on the integrity of understanding of the one preceding it. In Mathematics the technical terms for this is "compression" (after the work of Thurston) who coined the phrase to mean that concepts are compressed onto each other as a child's understanding in the subject grows.

It is virtually immoral to deny any child the right foundation on which they can build a true sense of numerical understanding in which they can "compress" new concepts. It short changes children to give them a strategy they can use to "apparently" obtain the correct answer without teaching the numerical understanding underpinning it. Surely they need a deep level of comprehension to make consistent and lasting progress. This approach also has the potential to send powerful subliminal messages that undertaking calculations with a minimal set of understanding and "tricks" is acceptable. Effective teaching is about meeting the needs of the individual child and there is therefore no place for giving some children simplified short term strategies that seemingly allow them to stay afloat in a given year group. The tragedy is that the lack of understanding that drives this approach will surface at some point in the future and where the foundations are not secure the children will sadly flounder in more complex concepts.

Whole School Strategy?

Research undertaken both within and outside the DfES with regard to the Numeracy Strategy has revealed that the overdevelopment of a range of methods sometimes does not allow children to securely consolidate any one consistent approach to calculation. Current thinking is that all schools should adopt a central core strategy and work out from this.

What are the advantages? A key factor is that where children are working on a similar problem with a similar structural basis they are more readily able to compare their working with their peers. This is because they do not have to decode or interpret their partner's strategy. Instead they can engage directly with the mathematical concepts underlying the calculation. This streamlines peer to peer discussion that can effectively build good mathematical understanding.

Having said that we should not limit children to the strategy we perceive as being the most appropriate. Whilst we might, from an adult perspective appreciate that a given strategy is both effective and efficient for a given calculation some children will inevitably revert to a strategy they feel most comfortable with. There is no shortcut here except that the teacher should exercise his/her professional judgement as to whether a child should continue with their own strategy or be "encouraged" to explore a more appropriate alternative.

The following are true scenarios from Key Stage 2:
i.   John understands the negative numbers in subtraction partitioning. So to solve a calculation such as 24-18 he takes 8 from 4 which leaves -4 and takes ten from twenty to make 10. This means he has 10-4 to calculate making the answer 6. He is secure in his knowledge and uses the strategy fluently. It is my contention therefore that he should be allowed to continue with this approach– unless the teacher perceives that in a fresh context his understanding may unravel or be undermined by the limiting nature of this particular strategy.
ii. Jane's desire to conquer the column method is parentally driven from home. She shows the teacher her method of decomposition for 232-178 and appears fluent in the strategy. However the teacher moves her on to the calculation 500 – 276. Apart from the fact that she is unable to get the correct answer the teacher soon becomes aware that there is little understanding of the value of the numbers for Jane. Her comprehension of what is happening to the numbers in this particular strategy is woeful. Encouraged to use the number line she was soon back on track with her understanding but interestingly enough she had

to regress to a point below that of her peers to rebuild her understanding in the fundamentals.

We should not negate the fact that children should have a wide range of strategies at their disposal. The number line strategy might act as a backbone throughout the school but over time children should learn to be discerning users of the strategy and should always look for the most "effective and efficient" method for any given calculation.

WILL THE "SLOW BOAT TO CHINA" LEAVE US UP A CREEK WITHOUT A PADDLE?

The Teaching Profession takes a "Slow Boat to China"

So Shanghai sits at the head of the 2012 PISA league tables (they are published every three years) and the only country to score over 600 points. This equates to three years' schooling above the OECD average. As we have seen in the past with Finland and other countries the great marketing machinery of "Educational Tourism" has wheeled into action as people flock to discover the secret of their success. I am not decrying the fact that teachers across the world seek to glean good pedagogy from others, indeed I have availed myself of two trips to Finland to do exactly the same but we should be wary of drawing conclusions from one country's performance no matter how exceptional it appears.

My clarion call for caution in this instance comes from the fact that one of the major conclusions being drawn from the Shanghai model of teaching is that their results, especially in Maths, rely heavily on the quality of their textbooks. This has placed the emphasis back on the textbook as the core feature of a successful curriculum. Even Tim Oates, Chair of the Expert Panel that reviewed the National Curriculum has waded in with his article

"Textbooks counts" including one section headed "The critical role of textbooks in maths pedagogy in Shanghai" One gets the feeling from the groundswell of rising opinion that if we just had great textbooks we would all achieve results in line with Shanghai. Put in a stark sentence like that one can see the absurdity of such a stance (and I am not for one minute inferring that Tim Oates or others of similar standing believe or indeed are saying this) but the teaching profession tends to lose things in translation and certainly I have heard many a teacher discuss the supposed value of "going back to textbooks"

As ever the answer is not to be found in the use of textbooks nor the lack of them but in pedagogy because as Dylan Wiliam reminds us "pedagogy trumps all". If we are to gain anything from the Shanghai experience then we need to extract the truth and meld it into secure pedagogy not cherry pick a few unrelated and philosophically shallow ideas and seek to string them together in the form of some semi-coherent classroom practice. I would take issue with the notion that textbooks, and their younger cousin – the worksheet, are going to take teaching and learning forward. As someone who believes that both teaching and learning should start with the child not with the content, I struggle to see how the textbook can therefore be the panacea to all our educational ills.

Bursting the Shanghai Bubble

Before we go overboard on the Shanghai success we must appreciate that it is data and all data can be skewed. The wise man is the one who uses data to pose questions not the one who uses it to find answers. So there are few things we should say about the "Shanghai success" that might set their scores in some form of context.

It has to be pointed out, as indeed it was by Xiang, a teacher from Shanghai who visited our school recently, that the scores relate only to one area of China and of course one of its most prosperous areas. If like all other countries in the PISA league table the scores for China overall were reported then there are some who believe that they might not maintain their elevated position. Andreas Schleicher, who runs the PISA programme, has encouraged other countries, specifically the UK, (TES 7th March 2014) to collate their own city data to make a fairer comparison. He did go on to concede that in his own opinion, even if London were lifted out of the UK it might still struggle to match the scores of Shanghai.

This factor is compounded by the socio-economic structure of Shanghai. China operates an internal registration programme called "Hukou" which prevents rural migrants from accessing urban public services and in particular, schools. Tom Loveless writes on this at length and is in correspondence with PISA about the inequality of the Shanghai system and its potential to skew international comparisons. He notes that the number of children without a Shanghai hukou at age 14 is less than 40% of the number one would expect for children of that age. In essence the education system within the city operates essentially as a selective system creaming off the elite and excluding the potentially less advantaged families from the rural areas. In September 2012 a fifteen year old Shanghai student, Zhan Haite undertook an internet campaign against the hukuo as she was forced to return to Jiangxi to attend High School because her parents were from that city. Even though she was born and educated in Shanghai the hukuo system is hereditary and is designed to lock a family's socio-economic status across generations.

This is further evidenced by Loveless in a table which shows Shanghai in bottom position, and indeed a total outlier for the expected percentage of 15 year olds to be found in the population. The lack of children in this age group, says Loveless, is a demonstration of the social engineering within the city. It is also true that whilst 84% of the high school graduates in Shanghai go to college this compares starkly with the 24% nationally.

As Xiang pointed out when he came to our school, each family is only allowed one child (although legislation now allows for two children, but only where the previous generation was from a single child family). This means that parents have the opportunity to plough all their energies and aspirations into a single child. Again this is compounded in Shanghai where parents spend an extortionate amount of money on tutoring and additional weekend activities. The average Shanghai family spends 49,000 yuan (£5,200) on tutors in the High school years, if one considers that the average wage in China is 42,000 yuan (£4,400) it is easy to see why the city's children make accelerated progress against their rural peers.

More interestingly is some research by Feniger (How to reason with PISA data) who found that Chinese students in Australia outperform the children in Shanghai. The students from a Chinese background in Australia scored an average of 615 in Maths compared to 613 for those living in Shanghai. The conclusion drawn by "Save Our Schools" was not that Shanghai excels but that "the top school results in east Asia were due to Confucian culture, homework, coaching and "tiger mothers". It may well be true that the cultural influences are stronger than the education system in one Chinese City. As Tim Dodd states in his article for the Financial Review such evidence does have the appearance of "casting doubt on the widely held assumption that teaching methods in Chinese schools are superior."

All of the above is not to decry or debunk Shanghai's success out of hand, that would be an unacceptable form of educational arrogance. In fact I applaud those who have visited the country seeking to glean inspiration from such a successful system. However there is a danger that we look at their success through superficial spectacles looking for quick wins in our desire to "Raise Standards" The above arguments are therefore given to counter this and encourage educationalists to look a little more deeply at what it is that allows certain schools to perform at such a high level. Certainly if we are going to lift the concept of using textbooks as a quick fix solution to all out mathematical ills then we need to temper such a simplistic approach with some of the arguments presented above.

Are Textbooks and Worksheets the answer?

As Tim Oates states in his article "there has been a conscious movement in England away from wide use of high quality textbooks" In fact only 10% of students in the UK have teachers who use textbooks as a basis for instruction compared with 70% in Singapore and 95% in Finland. As stated above just because a few high performing schools systems use textbooks does not mean this makes them the Holy Grail of educational achievement. As Oates accepts there are plenty of high performing systems, he quotes Massachusetts as one example, that does not have a central textbook focus and yet still outscore many jurisdictions.

All this and the above debate on Shanghai's scores draws us back to Dylan Wiliam's comment that "pedagogy trumps all". So if we are to use textbooks or worksheets then the rationale should be based on secure pedagogy not just centred on what the school down the road is doing, even if that school is seemingly successful and a few thousand miles away in a Chinese city .

So what is the pedagogical basis for learning?
The Wyche holds to a constructivist, child centric approach to learning. The key question therefore is how do teacher based worksheets fit into that pedagogy. For me worksheets muddy the learning waters on so many levels and I can only see a return to a teaching culture founded on them as a backward step. My concerns are numerous and are outlined below.

(i) Constructivism and the Locus of Control

True learning is undertaken by children themselves and occurs when they are placed in an arena where they can explore (or construct) learning in their own cognitive framework. In terms of Maths this belief should lead to a classroom that has many open ended tasks and where the focus will lean towards constant reasoning and dialogue as the children seek to develop mathematical concepts and the understanding behind them. The worksheet culture is virtually the antithesis of this.

Worksheets and textbooks have a natural tendency to focus the learning away from the child and back onto the teacher's agenda. This in turn creates a culture where the locus of control is held by the teacher rather than the learner. This sends out a powerful cultural message. For instance the worksheet that consolidates the number bonds to 10 poses the following thought in the child's mind; "I know the teacher has taught me these so I must now attempt to get them right just like she taught me" The blank sheet of paper with the question posed "How many ways can you find to make the number 10?" sends the message to the child that they are being trusted to explore this concept for themselves. The subliminal subtext is that the teacher believes they have the capability within themselves to demonstrate competency in this area. I choose to see this as giving the child "The Mantle of the Expert" The learning, and more importantly the concept of trusting the child to learn, is given to the child and empowers him to become a self-motivated learner. So whilst the results on the paper for the two activities may look virtually identical i.e. both pieces of paper will have the number bonds to 10 on them; the psychological difference in the mind of the child and the consequent impact on the classroom learning culture transmitted through the two approaches are poles apart.

(ii) The Glass Ceiling

Related to this, are the limitations that the worksheets place upon the child and their learning. Using the above example there would be nothing to stop a child writing 4.5 + 5.5 even if they were Year 2. The former approach prevents any such exploration by the child because the teacher has set the boundaries and they are rigidly determined by what the teacher thinks the child should do. Whilst this approach places limits on the learning of all children, it is especially stifling for the more able learner. Many have the ability to move beyond our own expectations if they were given an arena in which they could explore concepts at a deeper level. Also we all know that learning is not linear. For some children, in any given lesson, a concept may just click and suddenly they are able to achieve way ahead of their years for reasons no-one fully understands. The open ended task allows them to continue to learn at their new found pace.

(iii) Convergent and Divergent Thinking
The emphasis on performance causes the thinking in the classroom to become very narrow and convergent; this is the antithesis of everything we are trying to build in a thinking classroom. The child will start to live in a cultural bubble where they come to see the goal of each lesson as being able to "answer the questions at the end". Imagine a staff meeting where no-one was allowed home until they had answered ten questions at the end. Throughout the meeting your attention would be drawn away from the richness of pedagogical debate and down a track where you would be seeking to second guess what the questions might be from the tenure of the conversation and discussion so that you could go home on time. We cannot place children in a similar environment where the learning narrows and they focus on the questions that they will have to answer at the end.

(iv) Creativity
The beauty of the emergent approach is that it allows the children to explore Maths in its own right. They have the freedom to move around the Mathematical landscape exploring concepts on the way and developing their own understanding. The worksheet culture closes all this down, both for the teacher and the child. The teacher is aware that if the children are to complete the worksheet at the end of the lessons they must teach them the appropriate material to fulfil the task and at that point the lesson focus switches tangibly from child to curriculum content. For the child the lesson becomes a narrow activity, driven by the teacher towards the final end goal of the assessment questions. This will have a detrimental impact on both the teaching and learning.

(v) The Nature of Learning

The nature of learning is social in nature. Vygotsky's view was not just constructivism but very much "social constructivism" i.e. that we create our learning in a social arena alongside others. Neil Mercer points out that the most powerful tool for this is "talk". All learning should therefore take place in a social context that has peer to peer exploring as a focus. The worksheet predicates against this placing the child in a role where they are working in an individualised context and being asked for the right or wrong answer rather than exploring the full orb of learning in all its breadth.

Many would argue that the worksheet is not a learning tool but an assessment tool. If this is the case then by definition it cannot be used or seen as a powerful tool for learning. You cannot effectively assess something that you have not learnt so to give a child a worksheet on the principles of aerodynamics would not be useful without a lesson preceding it. Children need to have learnt the concept before they are tested on it. For this reason the worksheet is a very weak tool for learning although some might argue it is a powerful tool for assessment.

(vi) Assessment Tool

If one accepts that the worksheet is an assessment tool then how useful is it? The mantra from the teaching profession is that the results from the pen and paper tests of the SAT scores are unreliable. If this is the case then why should we assume that the pen and paper tests of the worksheet are any different? The assessment facility of the worksheet is limited to testing the knowledge in a given area not necessarily the understanding. As we have seen here at The Wyche in the past, there are children well into Key Stage 2 that can calculate 23% of 345 and yet don't fully appreciate the numerical process or indeed have understanding of the basic principles of percentages. Surely what we need to test is the understanding not simply the ability to calculate (though this may have its place on occasions). The challenge comes in designing a worksheet that demonstrates children's understanding. I would venture the opinion that it cannot be done and that even if it can, an alternative assessment tool such as an explanation either to the teacher, a peer or in written form, would be far more effective.

(vii) Right or Wrong?

If the focus of the worksheet is on the "testing" of what the child has been taught, this places the child in a black and white situation where they are either right or wrong. This again sends a powerful cultural message to the child, especially in Maths where, if we are not careful, the "answer" becomes the Holy Grail to be sought rather than the conceptual understanding that lies behind it. Whilst one cannot get away from the fact that there are always elements of the academic process where ideas are right or wrong, the learning journey should not be so clear cut. Learning works best in the land of the grey not the land of the black and white. Learning is "messy" and it involves a complexity of understanding and thinking that cannot be reduced down to a few questions on a piece of paper at the end of a lesson.

(viii) Right or Wrong By-product

A powerful by-product of the right or wrong culture generated by the worksheet is that it leaves children feeling emotionally vulnerable. Each child should be getting work wrong on a regular basis as without this I would question whether any learning is actually taking place. However we need to keep children on the journey where they see learning as a continual process of refinement and an expanding of their own knowledge and understanding. The hiatus caused by a worksheet given at the end of each lesson shifts the emphasis from continual learning to one of achievement and the requirement to succeed. It places the child in a position where they are more likely to focus on the successful completion of the task rather than the more holistic element of learning. This in turn will develop a performance rather than a learning culture in the classroom.

(ix)   Decoding of the Worksheet

As many have observed in working with the SAT papers, a child's ability to achieve is as much about decoding the worksheet as it is about understanding the curriculum concept being taught. There are many children who know the Maths but struggle to decode the context of a rather bland, 2-dimensional worksheet. We should be setting assessments in a richer, more holistic framework wherever possible.

Conclusion

In conclusion it is interesting to note that those who have visited Shanghai through the Maths Hub project return presenting a very different picture of teaching from the rather bland stereotype of children in rows working from textbooks. Whilst it is undoubtedly true that the textbook is a central feature within the teaching system, what teachers are more struck by is the reasoning that goes on within the class; the constant dialogue between teacher and child as they explore concepts at an ever increasing depth. This notion challenges the idea that the textbooks are the driving force behind the success. The mid-term report on the Shanghai exchange programme noted that "each lesson is designed in minute detail; each step choreographed; each question planned meticulously, and follow-up questions, according to a pupil's first response, also planned." I would suggest it is this focus on quality first teaching that is reaping the rewards not the narrowing and closing down of a curriculum driven by a set of multiplication calculations found on page 42.

ASSESSMENT WITHOUT LEVELS – WHERE TO NEXT?

Levels are no more!

So like the dodo before it, levels have become extinct. The onset of the new National Curriculum simultaneously brought the life of curriculum levels to an ignominious end. The dodo was hunted because its meat was considered a peculiar delicacy. Its disappearance meant that the hunter had to find an alternative diet. Teachers find themselves in a similar dilemma. Since their introduction National Curriculum levels have been the staple diet for schools to demonstrate progress to those who deem it necessary. Yet despite the fact that levels have gone, the accountability hunter still requires schools to demonstrate progress, and its insatiable appetite for data shows no sign of abating. So what are we to feed it on?

The demise of assessment levels will probably divide opinion within the teaching profession. There will be those who decry the fact that there is no longer any common language on which to base any discussion on assessment between schools. However the ubiquitous desire to coerce schools into demonstrating "good levels of progress" means many will be glad to see the back of a system that measured tenuous progress in the narrowest of curricula and based on a few tests at the end of a key stage. Of

course there will be many, a bit like myself whose sympathies straddle both viewpoints but wherever we sit on this continuum the teaching profession is left with the fundamental question:
Where do we go from here?

The Issue in focus

Whilst we would all love to believe that the abolition of levels is a step in a process to release schools from the overly bureaucratic system of accountability, the government is quite clear that tracking progress is not going away. So whilst the Secretary of State announced in May 2013 that "as part of our reforms to the national curriculum, the current system of 'levels' used to report children's attainment and progress will be removed. It will not be replaced." The later document 'Reforming Assessment and Accountability for Primary Schools' leaves schools in no doubt they will continue to be required to keep records of children's progress: "Schools should have the freedom to decide how to teach their curriculum and how to track the progress that pupils make' (DfE, 2014 p4)

So we enter a vacuum. There is no national system, nor any plans to formulate one in the near future. Instead schools are being asked to concoct their own assessment systems. So apart from the fact that it does not seem to be a good use of time and energy for 24,000 schools to do this individually, it might also be argued that it makes no sense to have 24,000 different tracking systems operating throughout the country.

Why have levels disappeared?

The "Expert Panel" were commissioned to revise the National Curriculum and after much deliberation decided to remove the concept of levels as an assessment framework for the new document.

In early discussions with colleagues, there seems to be the understanding that as levels were the primary means for tracking progress we need a system that operates as closely to that as is possible. It also appears to me that solutions are often being driven by the numerous software houses producing pupil tracking programs that love nothing more than to apply numbers to children that can then sit neatly in a coloured spreadsheet. As John Viner says "Schools are being seduced by commercial packages that simply offer levels by a different name" But if Alison Peacock is right when she says; "The idea you can put a number against a child's ability is flawed and dangerous" (Guardian, Sunday 25th March 2015) then maybe we should be looking to pedagogy to drive the changes not computer software.

We should take time therefore, to engage with the philosophy behind their demise and also with the rationale for their inclusion in the first place. There is a real danger that we invent something that resembles, and thereby contains all the foibles, of the old system. Similarly some of the "new" solutions being proposed are those that the profession jettisoned in the early days of the assessment debate. It does feel a little like we are playing out the old adage that; "the lesson we learn from history is that no-one learns the lesson from history"

The Rationale for the removal of levels

The rationale for the removal of levels is well documented and many educationalists have contributed to the debate. However it would appear that the main objections are as follows:

(i) Compensation Based Testing
Levels are calculated on a "compensation" basis especially when it comes to the SAT tests themselves. This means that children can score level 4 in a multiplicity of ways. Some children may attain level 4 through a breadth of understanding in pure level 4 concepts. However another child may pick up marks from level 5 questions and have blind spots on some areas of level 4

and yet score the same mark on the test. Another child may pick up marks on a completely different set of level 4 questions and have differing blind spots to the previous child. Yet all three students tumble out the end of the system being labelled as "level 4" As most of us know it is possible to attain level 4 on a SAT paper just by answering all the "number" questions. Therefore there may be children across the country (although I accept it is unlikely) who have no understanding of Shape, Space or Measure and yet are still deemed "level 4". So what does that tell us about the achievement of the child? In short very little, except they sit somewhere in a broad ability band that covers a two year span in terms of the National Curriculum.

(ii) Best Fit Models

In 1994 Ron Dearing was asked to slim down the assessment process. He drew up "Attainment Targets" which to all intents and purposes were the POS copied out with the words "Pupils should..." at the beginning. But they were collated and written in a succinct format that allowed teachers to undertake a process known as "Best Fit" to determine which level any child was functioning at. However this only led unwittingly to a furthering of the "compensation based" model.

(iii) The Threshold Issue

All schools will be aware that if a level at KS2 takes two school years then to have an assessment system with such a wide banding system will produce inevitable anomalies. We have children who scrape through the KS2 SAT test and score a level 4 on the lower limit of the threshold scores. Then similarly we had one child who in reply to the question "Round 4.79 to the nearest whole number" put "5.00" as the answer. This was marked wrong as the correct answer is simply 5. This single question prevented him achieving level 5 which he missed by one mark. It is evident to all that there is a chasm in ability between children but levels can mask this at times.

(iv) Ubiquitous sub-levelling

At their inception levels were introduced with the expectation that they would monitor a child's progress at the end of each Key Stage. There was never any expectation in national documentation that the levels would be broken down into the ubiquitous sub-levels that now proliferate in schools.

So what does a 3c look like? Well who is to know? Teachers struggle enough in moderating across the levels themselves let alone fine grading within them. Most teachers consider a 3c child to be one who is secure in the concepts of level 2 and has taken on board a minimal amount of concepts at level 3 but is secure in few of them. In short they are working at level 3 but are not level 3 so the assumption is that they must therefore be 3c. So what is a 3b? Traditionally it has been viewed as depicting an average level 3 child but how can they be labelled as level 3 if they can still move on to 3a which presumably contains concepts in which they are not yet secure. This feeds back into the compensation debate above. Which areas are they not secure in? It may not be the same as their peers. Surely the 3a child is the average level 3 child because they are the only one who is secure in all the level 3 concepts and can therefore be the only child who can claim to be fully "level 3"

(v) Stages in Monitoring Progress

If the statutory requirement was always to use levels simply at the end of a Key Stage how have we ever ended up with a system that monitors progress in such short time spans? Sadly we went from assessing children every Key Stage to every year, then to every half year, then to every term and I know of one school that is in "Requires Improvement" that is being asked to demonstrate progress every half term. One may be able to monitor progress every 6 weeks (although somehow I doubt it) but a curriculum level that spans two years of a child's academic life is going to be a very blunt instrument to do it with. In two years there are 12 half terms. In theory if we are to demonstrate progress we would need 12 sub-divisions in each level. So much for 3a, 3b and 3c bring on 3h and 3k!

(vi) Levelling work or children

The levels were also designed to assess the child not pieces of work. The first sentence in the Level 4 attainment target for writing in the National Curriculum 2000 stated that: "Pupil's writing in a range of forms is lively and thoughtful" How do you judge that from one piece of work? The answer is you can't and were never intended to. Yet throughout the land teachers can be heard debating whether "This is a level 3 piece of writing". To be fair APP went some way to acknowledging this by seeking to ensure teachers drew work from a range of genres but it hasn't stopped the profession focusing on the micro elements of individual contributions from the child rather than looking at the macro element of the child as a learner, or in this instance, as a writer.

(vii)   Levels as targets

In the drive to "raise standards" crossing the threshold of a level became a target to aim towards and put "undue pace" (Tim Oates' phrase) into the system. This led teachers, at times, to take shortcuts in understanding or leave behind elements of breadth so as to focus on areas that would allow the children to attain the next level. No-one needs me to tell them that this aspect intensifies around Year 2 and Year 6, but it is regrettable at any stage in a child's schooling. In fairness to schools, it is the system not the individual school that drives this but this only serves to make its use even more depressing.

(viii)   Moderation

Once we throw in the aspect of moderation we may begin to wonder why levels were ever invented at all. A few years ago we became involved with another school helping a younger teacher with her KS2 moderation of writing. There were some pieces she believed were level 6. We felt they were very much level 5. We were both being moderated and therefore were able to show the pieces from the other school to our moderator. He was in full agreement with our assessment. However a different moderator upon arriving at the other school declared them all to be secure level 6. The point is if we struggle as teachers to moderate, then what hope do we have when the moderators can't moderate.

The Rationale for the instigation of levels

In reading all of the above one might be forgiven for wondering why levels were ever conceived in the first place. However at their conception they had a clear rationale which for the most part was founded on secure pedagogy.

In 1988 the TGAT (Task Group on Assessment and Testing) was commissioned to develop an assessment framework which could run alongside the national curriculum. They created the concept of levels which were based on two key principles.

The first principle was that the system should produce a structure where all children could be seen to be progressing through the curriculum. Many models were explored including an age related scale score (these are frighteningly similar to those proposed by some schools now). This would mean that children at each age could be graded within their particular age band. However the child who scored Grade E in year 1 is likely to score Grade E in year 2. Indeed for some children it is quite easy to imagine a scenario where a child might be graded as such throughout their school career. This has the potential to have a devastating impact on their self-esteem. The levels were seen as a means in which all children could progress through the curriculum.

The second guiding principle was related to this and came from Carol Dweck's work on the "fixed" and "growth" mindsets. Paul Black (the group's main author) wanted to ensure that no child was locked into a self-fulfilling prophecy of always scoring a grade E at the end of each year. His contention was that this fostered a fixed mindset. The framework of levels presented children with the opportunity to set their own targets. So even if you were "Working Towards" at Year 2 you may well set yourself the target of attaining level 1 by Year 4. This thinking feeds straight into the "growth mindset" principle.

He also wished to make sure that the levels were "criterion referenced" rather than "norm referenced"; meaning that children would be levelled against the criteria outlined in the curriculum rather than being referenced within their peer group. This again allowed for the nurturing of a growth mindset preventing the same child always seemingly appearing at the bottom of the class. Assessment against criteria allows all children to make progress, albeit at different rates.

Above all Paul Black's belief was that assessment should have a formative rather than summative focus. As has been said many times: "You don't make a pig fatter by weighing it all the time" and so it is no surprise to find that he recommended that: "The basis of the national assessment system should be essentially formative, but designed also to indicate where there is need for more detailed diagnostic assessment. (Paragraph 27)

History will record that after the TGAT report many schools went down a route of ticking off every attainment target and every statement found in the Programmes of Study (POS) against individual children. I would suggest that this benefitted the makers of marker pens more than the children these assessments were meant to serve. In the current curriculum there are nearly 70 separate statements (depending on how you count them) in the Year 6 POS for Maths alone so in a class of 30 there would be 2,100 boxes for the teacher to tick. Surely life is too short for such things!

With the Dearing "best fit" model and the joys of APP behind us we now enter the uncharted waters of a life without levels. So how do we assess children in a manner that allows them to remain confident, ongoing learners yet couched in a recording system that delivers to external stakeholders.

Assessment Without Levels: What are we doing at The Wyche?

As with all things in education it is only by looking at the big picture that one can see the truth of what needs to be done and then the task of schools is to convert that into daily practice. So what is the big picture?

If we are to explore a cogent way forward we need to start by drawing a clear distinction between the two fundamental forms of assessment.

Formative assessment operates in every classroom in the land. It is complex because, as we all know, "learning is messy" and requires a high level of professional expertise to ensure that the daily judgements of children's progress are fed into their learning the following day. The other is summative assessment. All are agreed that the latter has little bearing on a child's ability to learn more effectively however it fulfils a completely different purpose which the system dictates is necessary. Employers need to know standards of those they are employing so we have GCSEs and A-levels. Ministers have decided that we need to be able to compare schools so they have invented SATs and league tables.

A Continued Focus on Formative Assessment

At the Wyche we have decided (and indeed always have) to focus clearly on formative assessment. I have never truly been interested in whether a child is 3c, 3b or 3a (except when drawing up data for external users) what I am more interested in is whether the child knows what to do in their lesson tomorrow to take their learning forward. Is it important for a teacher to know that a child who is not using full stops cannot be level 2 or is it more important that they know a good strategy for showing the child why they are needed in their writing?

The key is to focus on the next step of the learning journey not on what level the children are at. There is plenty of time at the end of the year to sit down and see where children have got to. However when I enter discussion with some schools it is almost as if they have reached a point where the focus is so data driven they appear to have subliminally imbibed a perceived truth that if the data is good then the teaching and learning must be good. This leads to the corollary that if we can improve the data through robust target setting then we will by definition improve the teaching. The words "cart" and "horse" spring to mind but more importantly I tend to observe that successful schools focus on the teaching and learning and let the data take care of itself.

Rather than using level thresholds as target markers I have always viewed levels as mileposts on a journey. If you walk from my home town of Ledbury across the hills to Malvern you will reach the village of Eastnor on the way. Upon arriving and looking at the map you will realise that you are nearly half way on your journey, it is simply a point you have naturally reached as part of your journey. However there has become a perverseness in the education system that sees us turn a simple milepost to be walked past into a staging post to be reached as quickly as possible. Therefore (so the educational parallel goes) if we can get to Eastnor quicker we will get to Malvern quicker. However we all know that just as athletes who sprint the first 10 miles of a marathon may well be out in front at some point they rarely end up winning the race in the end. This is also true of learning; those children that are accelerated through their conceptual understanding are not best served for learning in the long term because the foundations are rarely built with enough depth on which to build.

If a school focuses on the formative element of assessment then levels become a defunct construct. Tim Oates cites Wroxham Primary as a school that does not use levels. Alison Peacock in her article Life without levels wrote; "At The Wroxham School, a primary school, we have not talked to children and parents about 'levels' for the last ten years" In this regard The Wyche would claim the same because with the exception of the statutory requirement to report on levels in Year 2 and 6 there is no mention of levels anywhere else in the school. The conversation with children and parents relates to a child's next steps in their learning and there is no child anywhere in the school that would have any idea what level they were functioning at within the assessment framework of the National Curriculum.

So in terms of the quality of teaching, learning and assessment the government's edict regarding levels will have little impact on our school. The truth is no-one learns by knowing where they are up to now, they learn by understanding what they need to do next.

Wot! No Levels Anywhere!

However I am intrigued by Tim Oates' assertion that Wroxham does not use levels because when I log onto their data dashboard I can clearly see that 94% of the children attained level 4 in Maths. So what does he mean that they don't use levels?

The truth is they use them because at some point the purity of pedagogy hits the impurity of the accountability machine and that dances to the beat of a different drum. At this point in the debate we leave all thoughts of ongoing, effective teaching and learning behind and instead turn to making a judgement on outcomes. I am aware that schools are required to be accountable and therefore am fully cognisant of the need to deliver in these areas. However... we must never confuse the task of formatively assessing children as a key feature of learning with the task of assessing the outcomes of that teaching and pretending they are the same thing. Tim Oates rightly points out that this is one of the flaws historically with assessment as it "was introduced for one purpose but is now used for something else"

Here we get to the nub of the whole debate about levels and their disappearance. Whilst I might agree with many of the reasons for removing levels from the assessment framework the truth is that it is only the imposition of the accountability framework upon them that skews them and places them out of kilter. Of course schools can teach without levels there are plenty of schools that do. However, the accountability question relates to how schools demonstrate that children are making progress to an Ofsted team that are only in a school for a couple of days and that is a different issue entirely.

Dylan Wiliam makes an interesting point that is relevant to this argument. He believes that "Most solutions on offer are really recording systems not assessment systems" (Planning Assessment without Levels – Teach Primary) In truth we all know that genuine assessment is simply "a crucial part of effective teaching" (Reforming Assessment and Accountability DfE) whereas placing a score on a spreadsheet has no impact on learning whatsoever. So in this sense formative assessment is that on-going daily evaluation undertaken to inform teaching whilst summative assessment (or should we call it "summative recording" for clarity) is simply putting a marker in the sand as to where a child has reached at any given point in time. One looks forward to where a child needs to go next the other looks back at where a child has come from. It doesn't take much to work out which is the most effective in terms of learning for the child.

If we accept the premise that levels or any progress measure is only necessary to feed the accountability machine then it makes no sense to spend inordinate amounts of time developing an assessment system of any complexity. We should instead be maximising our time looking at the nuances and complexities of formative assessment which we know through John Hattie's research has a major impact on true learning.

It would be fair to say that at The Wyche we have spent less time than most engaging with the debate about "What a level 3 looks like" In truth it has always been of secondary importance to me. If you think about it there is no particular benefit to either the school or the teacher and even less to the child that their teacher is able at one glance to accurately determine the level of a given piece of work. The driver behind this approach has been national government who are the only ones interested in effective moderation because it makes for more accurate league tables. For myself I am not that interested in "beating the school down the road" in fact I know of few schools that are, we simply want to do the best for the children in our care and yet as a profession we have spent many training hours satisfying the desire of the system for accurate levels. So instead of this we ploughed hours of training into looking in depth at the elements of good teaching and learning that take children's learning forward. As we enter a post-levels era no-one now cares what a "level 3" looks like because they no longer exist and it is schools that focused on learning that find themselves in a potentially stronger position to move their children forward.

So we will therefore be developing a simple system that looks very much like levels because as Paul Black stated in 1988 they provide a progression framework for all children and allow staff to calibrate criterion-based standards easily. It will focus on the yearly programmes of study and each child will be graded within that year band with an a,b,c score, similar to those we have used for levels. This means that at KS2 instead of two levels we will have four with a level spanning a single year rather than the traditional two. We will use these to track progress using a best fit model. The children will continue to have no idea what "level" they are on and parents will continue to be informed of their child's progress against curriculum statements and the next steps of learning their child needs to take.

MASTER AND MISS: WILL MASTERY LEAD TO MISSERY?

Preface

In the relentless and seemingly endless journey to "raise standards" the next train to roll into the DfE station is the 7.52 to Mastery which will no doubt be stopping at a school near you on its journey towards its ultimate destination of educational excellence.

So what is mastery? According to the Oxford dictionary it is a *"comprehensive knowledge or skill in a given subject".* I am assuming the government cannot expect that the introduction of the word into the educational vocabulary will cause teachers to slap their foreheads, cry "doh" and wonder why they hadn't already been trying to move children towards a position of gaining "comprehensive knowledge" already. Of course teachers have always striven for excellence in children it is part of the DNA that causes them to enter the profession. So if the debate is not about semantics, what is the rationale behind the current initiative?

The current conceptual understanding of mastery has been "borrowed" from the Asian countries with an especial focus on the area of Mathematics.

The government, noting that our scores in the PISA league tables show a great disparity with many of the countries in the Far East, have looked at their teaching principles and sought to elucidate those that would benefit students in England. They have noted that these "successful" countries use a form of teaching known as "mastery". So Nick Gibb the school's minister is encouraging the teaching *profession "to learn from teachers in one of the best systems in the world (Shanghai), and implement teaching for mastery in your schools" (Speech on Maths Reform 27th March 2015)*. A message he repeated in his speech "The purpose of Education" (9th July 2015) when he stated *"England is now raising standards by helping primary schools to deliver the highly effective Asian-style mastery approach"*

The government's present understanding of the mastery pedagogy hinges on the belief that standards can be raised in all children if they are taught corporately as a whole class. This is an element they believe lies at the core of the Asian success, due to a greater emphasis on whole class teaching in these countries. So the new curriculum states that; *"The expectation is that the majority of pupils will move through the programmes of study at broadly the same pace"* The emphasis then becomes one based on teaching depth in a given idea rather than progressing the more able onto new concepts. This is a radical departure from the heavily differentiated curriculum that schools have been challenged to implement in recent years under the "personalised agenda." If this is the new dawn of educational enlightenment then it begs the obvious question: Why have we not seen all this before? Well, the simple answer is: We have.

The Historical Background

The concept of mastery is not new. Indeed, many of its principles date back to Aristotle and the other ancient Greek philosophers. But leaving ancient history aside, a reincarnation of the theory surfaced in the early years of the 20th century through the work of Washburne (1922) and it became popular in many American schools at this time. However, the real impetus came through the work of Benjamin Bloom in the 1980's. Whilst he is more well known for the "Bloom's Taxonomy" his major work came in pioneering the mastery principle and indeed it is his theory that the DfE cite in their own rationale for developing mastery.

Bloom noted that the "conventional" (his word) method of teaching involved teaching a class of 30 a given concept at the end of which the children would be assessed on what they had learnt. The results from any assessment tasks would logically result in a customary bell curve distribution based on the fact that some children would attain higher levels of understanding than others with the majority of children clustering around a centre point. However Bloom noted that earlier research by Anania (1981) and Burke (1983) had compared progress of children taught in a "conventional" class of 30 with the progress of those taught in a one-on-one tutoring situation. They found that the one to one scores were two standard deviations above the control class i.e. 98% of the students outperformed the control class.

From such data he wrote *"My major conclusion is: What any person in the world can learn almost all persons can learn if provided with appropriate prior and current conditions of learning"* In this he was challenging the current educational thinking of the day, which was based on a fixed view of academic ability. Bloom believed that this placed a glass ceiling on children's ability and that with the right learning environment all children could achieve to the same level. Acknowledging that one-to-one tuition "is too costly for most societies to bear on a large scale" he set about exploring how he could close this two standard deviation gap between the two teaching styles.

In 1984 he published his seminal *work "The 2 Sigma Problem: The Search for Methods of Group Instruction as Effective as One-to-One Tutoring."* Whilst he acknowledged that he was unable to replicate the two standard deviation of individual tutoring he did claim that "The average student under mastery learning was about one standard deviation above the average of the control class" He believed that over time 80% of the mastery students could achieve what the top 20% achieved with conventional class teaching. Pictorially it was represented in the following graph:

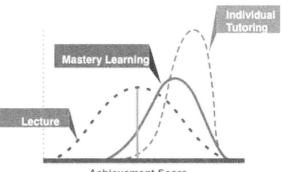

Achievement Score

His philosophy was underpinned by one important concept which revolved around time. The prevailing thinking in his day was that academic ability was innate and therefore fixed. So a teacher's assessments after a unit of work on a given concept would show that some children had achieved well and others less well. The explanation for this would be down to the fact that some children had natural ability that allowed them to move faster through the material than those who struggled to take the concepts on board. Bloom sought to challenge this and offered an approach that was a paradigm shift in thinking. He reasoned that if it was possible through individual tutoring for children to attain similar standards to the control group then the issue cannot lie in the child's intelligence it must rely in the teaching style.

Working on this premise he developed a teaching model that kept the curriculum constant and made time the fluid element; whereas traditional teaching keeps time constant and allows pupils' 'mastery' of curriculum content to vary. Mastery learning keeps learning outcomes constant but varies the time needed for pupils to become proficient or competent at these objectives. On the basis of this he divided the curriculum into a series of concepts to be learnt. These were then taught to the children, not in a given time frame but taught until all the children had acquired the concept. For those who achieved this earlier than others they would move on to extension material that would develop depth in the concept before moving on to new material which once again would be introduced to the class as a whole.

In short Bloom's differentiation was not based on what the children had achieved because he believed *"slower learners do succeed in attaining the same criterion of achievement as the faster learners... they (just) learnt with more time and help than was given to the others"* Carroll, another forerunner in the principles of mastery, concurred with Bloom saying *"aptitude is a measure of learning rate, i.e. a measure of the amount of time the student would require to learn a given level under ideal instructional conditions"*

The acceleration in learning was down to one key factor. Bloom noted that the key to learning in the tutorial sessions was related to the instant feedback that the student received. As soon as mistakes were made they were corrected and therefore erroneous learning was not allowed to take root. Bloom's premise was that *"group instruction produces errors in learning at each stage – no matter how effective a teacher is"* So the key for Bloom was that *"teachers and students reveal the errors in learning shortly after they occur... (and that) appropriate correctives are then introduced"* This he says is *"the essence of mastery learning strategy: group instruction and individualised help as students need it"*

Initially Bloom suggested that weaker students required approximately 10-15% additional time to achieve the same results as their peers but in later research he suggested that over time the gap closed *"so that students became more and more similar in their learning rate until the difference between fast and slow learners becomes very difficult to measure"*

Can it all be that simple?

I suspect that any discerning reader will have asked themselves the obvious question; if it is this straight forward why are we only just implementing this style of teaching now?

As with all research, Bloom's findings are hotly disputed. Before we turn to the dissenters it is worth noting, in the name of impartiality, that there are many supporters of Bloom's work but the dissenting voice is fairly strong. The greatest of these was probably Slavin. Interestingly he agreed with the principles of mastery and lauded the concept of providing secure and robust feedback for students but to his initial surprise his own research failed to support the notion of dramatic academic gains. He found that when the philosophy was dropped into a whole class setting that *the "group based mastery learning has modest to non-existent effects on student achievement"* In a later article he sought to qualify his view saying *"my critics imply that I am opposed to mastery teaching in principle. I'm not... my only quarrel is with group based mastery learning... the year-long study showed no greater effects for mastery learning than traditional methods on standardised measures"*

The Sutton Trust produces documents related to the current thinking on educational research but even they remain healthily sceptical of the gains that mastery teaching claims to elucidate. In their EEF toolkit they note that; *"There is a large quantity of research on the impact of mastery learning, though much of it is relatively dated and findings are not consistent"* One of the EEF projects into mastery concluded that; *On average, Year 1 pupils in schools adopting Mathematics Mastery made a small amount more progress than pupils in schools that did not. However, the effect detected was not statistically significant, meaning that it is not possible to rule out chance as an explanation."* They also quote Slavin saying that there was *"little evidence that effects are maintained over time"*

So where does that leave the debate?

I am happy to leave the academics to argue over the validity of research results. My main concern is to evaluate the philosophy underpinning the government's current move towards encouraging schools towards mastery teaching, especially in Maths where it really seems to have taken hold through the work of the Maths Hubs and the Shanghai-English project being funding by the DfE.

My instinctive reaction to the mastery debate is to pose the obvious question that every classroom practitioner would ask: *How is it possible to teach the full span of abilities in one class lesson without dumbing down content for the more able or losing the less able in a morass of challenging concepts?*

The complexity in the debate comes in the fact that the DfE have married a philosophical concept to the teaching style adopted in some countries on the other side of the globe and unfortunately the two cannot always co-habit successfully. It is evident to me that whilst the mantra from government is *"Mastery is the model of the high-performing Asian systems such as Shanghai, Singapore and South Korea. It delivers a meticulous approach to arithmetic (through) whole class teaching" (Nick Gibb's speech on Maths Reform 2015)* this is slightly disingenuous on two counts. Firstly, as I will shortly, show the teachers in Shanghai are not class teaching all the time but have provision for children at both ends of the academic spectrum. Secondly to call "whole class teaching" mastery is not something that Bloom advocated. Even he concluded that there would always a small percentage of children in any class who would not be able to access a class based lesson. So in both the case of replicating Shanghai and in the purity of the mastery model the current mantra being delivered falls well short.

So what is the truth?

(i) Bloom's Theory

I believe Bloom's work has much to commend it. He was advocating what Carol Dweck came to articulate later as a "growth mindset" and in many ways he was ahead of his time in this regard. His research took place in the days prior to all the brain research we have access to these days. So whilst we now know that the brain has greater plasticity to learn than anyone previously thought it would now appear that Bloom's ideas were prophetic in nature. He was right to challenge the assumption of the fixed mindset and definitely right to challenge the notion that intelligence was innate.

He was also right in his assumption that feedback is the key to successful learning. Again something that John Hattie in his meta-analysis study "Visible Learning" came to conclude many years later. Once again Bloom was ahead of his time - a forerunner to Wiliam and Black's "Inside the Black Box" and all of Shirley Clarke's work on formative assessment that followed it. Thomas Guskey, an advocate of Bloom's work said *"a far better approach, according to Bloom, is for teachers to use their classroom assessments as learning tools, both to provide students with feedback on their learning progress and to guide the correction of learning errors"*

For Bloom the issue was never about "whole class" teaching in many ways it was the antithesis of this. He was more interested in replicating the principles of "individual tutoring" albeit in a "whole class" setting. So far from advocating teaching the class as a whole he was proposing a balance of whole class teaching underpinned, and more especially driven by, an individualised programme of feedback and learning that supported the child. This is somewhat different from the current message being delivered which leaves many with the feeling that differentiation is a thing of the past and that teaching the class with uniform content is the way forward. Slavin's criticism of Bloom is relevant here, you will remember he was critical not of the concept of mastery but critical of its use in a "group setting". Slavin's critics take him to task not because of his findings but because he limited his study to "whole group settings". I don't wish to draw conclusions from an "argument of silence" but it would appear that those supporting Bloom did not argue with his conclusions they just argued with the fact that his research was skewed through selectivity. But this does leave us with the question; is mastery teaching appropriate in a whole class setting?

Certainly Bloom acknowledged that there were some in the school population who could not access the whole class element of the curriculum. He put the number at 2-3% of the population. We may wish to argue over the percentage but the truth is that even he acknowledged that additional provision needed to be made for these children. The other aspect aligned to this was his assertion that he recognised that there would always be children that would need "additional time" to acquire concepts. Indeed this was the key principle of his theory in the sense that he saw "time taken" as the differentiating factor rather than the material delivered in the class. He wrote; *"Using the concept of mastery teaching I sought to find ways in which the slower learners could be given the extra time and help they needed, outside of the regular class schedule"* He was quite clear that whole class teaching would not suffice to make the progress required for these children and that additional support outside the lesson, or intervention as we might call it, would be a necessary part of the learning process. It is therefore disingenuous to claim, as many do presently, that all children can make progress within the one class lesson. Bloom did not expect this nor (as we shall see) do the teachers in Shanghai.

Bloom's work has been seen by many modern commentators as a potential solution to the thorny issue of social mobility. At present the link between low socio-economic background and poor educational attainment is greater in the UK than in almost any other developed country. However if Bloom is correct in his findings then mastery teaching should be able to close that gap, accelerating the progress of the less able and allowing them to function academically alongside their peers. It may well be the case that mastery teaching will close the gap but one must be sure that this apparent increasing congruence has not come at the expense of suppressing the attainment of the more able pupils. I know Bloom builds extension material into his teaching model and along with every educationalist I laud the government's intention to focus on depth of understanding rather than the linear race to see who can reach the level 6 finishing line. In truth I have yet to meet a teacher who thought that pushing children on rather than broadening and enriching their conceptual understanding was ever a good idea in the first place. However I am now assuming schools will be judged in league tables on the depth of a child's learning in a limited number of concepts rather than on how many concepts they have acquired. The pedagogy is faultless but its assessment presents a huge challenge. It is a lot easier to assess linear concepts through a simple "Have they got it?" style of question rather than to try to tease out the differing levels of understanding children may have within a given concept especially when the assessment is limited to a pencil and a piece of paper.

Related to this I am intrigued by comments in the NCETM's document on mastery. For instance it states: *Taking a mastery approach, differentiation occurs in the support and intervention provided to different pupils, not in the topics taught, particularly at earlier stages.* The issue I have with a comment like this is not what is said, but what is not said. If the topics can remain the same at "earlier stages" then it seems to infer (through its silence if nothing else) that as the children move into Year 6 where breadth of content becomes more disparate it may be harder, (or undesirable? – again it doesn't say) to continue to maintain teaching every topic to every child. Of course this can be done but my question would be: *Does this come at a cost to those children at either ends of the academic spectrum?*

I am not here either to slate the work of Bloom or the implications people draw from it as I said earlier his ideas have much to commend them, what I am seeking to discern is whether his work dovetails into the current mantra that schools are imbibing from central government. As Roy Blatchford wrote in his article in the Guardian *"Differentiation is out. Mastery is the new classroom buzzword"* So has differentiation disappeared from the classrooms in England never to be seen again, confined to the museum of historical educational initiatives?

All I am saying is when I read Bloom's work I see he has a group that cannot access the "whole class" lesson, he has an intervention group that are offered extra support from an "aide" (his word for a teaching assistant I assume) and the rest of the class are taught together in similar fashion to the that advocated by the Numeracy Strategy of 1999 with a differentiated curriculum for the more able that looks at depth and understanding of the concept rather than a linear progression through the curriculum. All this being underpinned by a secure understanding and outworking of powerful formative assessment in a class based environment. Sounds ideal to me! But it is not what is currently being sold to us by the powers at be who claim Shanghai is the answer to all our ills.

(ii) Shanghai

Most of what I have read about the Shanghai system, admittedly from sources in this country, relates to its focus on "whole class teaching" and to "Mastery" teaching. As I have sought to articulate above I have struggled to quite square the circle regarding the issue of the whole class lesson and when Xiang a teacher from Shanghai came to visit our school I sought clarification from him on how the principle of differentiation operates in his country. The quotes are taken directly from his email.

(i)   Whilst he acknowledges what we already know, that each lesson is 35 minutes long and that (in his words) *"most of the students can follow the teacher's teaching and requirements"* he then goes on to clarify this by saying that this is *"because in the class, there are no students who need to take special care"*

(ii) Unlike the impression given by many pushing the "whole class Shanghai" message Xiang states that *"After lessons, teachers will give the weaker students face to face teaching to help them catch other students."* This is in line with Bloom's mastery model of course and there can be no doubt that this will be a powerful element in the child's learning and subsequent progression.

(iii) Finally Xiang dispels the rather dewy eyed version of Shanghai classes where everyone is seemingly at the same level and content to be there when he says *"however, not all students can achieve the same level or score in examinations. Teachers have different expectations for different students, but they hope their students can do their best to learn."*

I have no qualms with the Shanghai system. Why should I? A system where SEN provision is seemingly catered for, weaker children have tutorials with their classteacher and teachers recognise that not all children have the same ability and therefore set different expectations for them. But this is not the message we are getting from the powers at be – the mantra is that Chinese children are taught uniformly in one class for 35 minutes. Well they are to a certain extent, but so were children when the Numeracy Strategy first came out but it is not the whole story.

The other factor to be considered is the cultural element. In a country where every family has but one child to dote on, where family support is high and the money spent on tutoring outside school by the middle classes exceeds the average wage of the poor in the rural areas, it is little surprise to find academic standards thrive. One study found that Asian children in Australia and New Zealand were scoring higher in PISA scores than those back in their home countries, which again only seeks to lend itself to an interpretation that the cultural impact is very high. It is not always easy to transport or translate pedagogy that is culturally defined into other settings. It is similar to that tacky trinket you bought on your Spanish package holiday last year, it seemed such a great purchase when you were in the Mediterranean sunshine after a few glasses of sangria but get it home and you suddenly find the reason why recycling bins were invented. The principle is that not everything that appears good in one country will transpose seamlessly across cultures.

What do we conclude?

At a recent conference I took the opportunity in one of the breaks to engage the speaker who was sharing under the auspices of the DfE. I was challenging the notion that the whole class teaching model she was advocating was sound pedagogical practice. It was only in this one to one setting that she admitted that children in Shanghai were taught outside the whole class teaching time, either for support or for extension work set for homework. I pleaded with her not to be so disingenuous with her messages.

I believe we are in danger of having schools seeking to flow in what they think is a pedagogically secure current only to find themselves drifting towards an educational waterfall with a perilous drop at the end as children on either end of the spectrum struggle to access a curriculum that is appropriate to their needs. As far as I can see the non-differentiation pedagogy being touted by many is based neither on mastery nor on the Shanghai system. Therefore we need to look more critically at what these offer and only integrate the best practice from each into our schools. I do believe the present message falls short on all levels and will leave both teachers and children frustrated as they seek to adopt a system that may well be flawed at its inception.

Postscript: Is differentiation important?

I leave you with a quote from Roy Blanchford's article I quoted from earlier.
In his memoir, An Intelligent Person's Guide to Education, former Eton headmaster Tony Little recounts the delightful story of workmen at the

school uncovering fragments of a wall painting under some wood panelling. The images, from around 1520, are believed to be the earliest representation of a school scene in England. A banner headline from Roman scholar Quintilian crowns the scene "Virtuo preceptoris est ingeniorum notare discrimina", meaning "the excellence of the teacher is to identify the difference in talents of students". In a word; differentiation!

WHAT ON EARTH IS SPIRITUALITY?

Life isn't about the number of breaths we take,
but the moments that take our breath away.
Anonymous

What on earth is Spirituality?

The National Curriculum states as one of its two core aims that each school should *"aim to promote pupils' **spiritual**, moral, social and cultural development."* The Wyche Curriculum also speaks of, *"developing a sense of spirituality"* within children. Being the head of a Church of England school with a contingent of foundation governors drawn from a highly supportive and active church I felt that working on such a theme would be relatively straightforward, however...

I rapidly discovered that a clear understanding of the concept of spirituality itself was as tricky as nailing jelly to a wall. It appeared that the more we thought the more confused we became. I was comforted by two people who had trod this path before us.

The first was Archbishop Temple who was asked to produce a statement on spirituality for the Education Reform Act of 1944. Having grappled with the inclusion of religion and establishing little consensus he turned to his assistant Canon Hall for advice. Hall reflected on his solution sometime later saying ; *"The churches were in such a state at the time that we thought if we used the word spiritual they might agree to that because they did not know what it was"*. I felt comforted that if the Archbishop of Canterbury and the churches throughout the land were struggling to define the concept then a humble Headteacher such as myself ought not to feel too discouraged.

The second crumb of comfort came from Jenny; a ten year old child quoted in David Hay's book, *The Spirit of the Child*. Jenny was reflecting on the fact that she found deep meaning in some of the hymns sung within the school, however she went on to explain; *"You think it's quite easy when you are singing it but when you try and explain it you don't know which words to use."*

It would appear whether you are a child, an Archbishop or a Headteacher that the concept of spirituality, especially when defining it in a school setting, is not as simple as it might first appear.

Schools however, are charged with a statutory obligation as determined by the National Curriculum, to provide for a child's spiritual development. The 1944 act stated that it was the *"duty of the local education authority for every area, so far as their powers extend, to contribute towards the spiritual, moral, mental, and physical development of the community"*. In 1988 the new education reform act continued to promote *"the **spiritual**, moral, cultural, mental and physical development of pupils at the school and of society;"* Recent curriculum changes have placed the responsibility for children's spiritual development away from the local authority and onto the local school stating that *"the school curriculum should promote pupils' spiritual, moral, social and cultural development"* (National Curriculum

2000) On a broader scale the UN charter for human rights also refers to spirituality four times, so on every level it remains incumbent upon all schools, not just church schools, to ensure they are nurturing the spiritual needs of the children in their care.

What is the problem of Spirituality in Schools?

As Archbishop Temple proved it is hard to gain consensus on the meaning of spirituality in a church setting, therefore we should not be surprised to find that those in a secular setting (which most schools are) struggle even more when they seek to embed it into their curriculum. It would appear to me that there are two key issues that impinge greatly upon this and each relates to the personal stance teachers take in coming to the subject.

Our current, post-modern society has become increasingly secular in recent years and it would therefore be rare, to find a school where each member of the staff had a strong faith and a clear framework in which to develop a cogent spiritual curriculum. For instance, how can someone who does not believe in God lead an assembly on the power of God in creation, without feeling they are undermining their own integrity? Those who find themselves in this position often feel disempowered to lead children, and resort to leading assemblies that have a generic moral context. Whilst they are certainly worthwhile and instil a sense of morality into the school ethos they do lack the ability to advance the spiritual development of the child.

On the other hand there are those who have a strong faith themselves, especially where their faith aligns itself with the denominational foundation of their school. It is often assumed such teachers have an advantage when it comes to implementing a spiritual curriculum. However, children are young, and in that sense vulnerable, and whilst it is right for schools to present a clear spiritual framework in which to explore faith it is wholly inappropriate for any school to use its position to indoctrinate or coach children in a given belief. So for those with a faith the converse challenge arises to their secular colleagues, namely, how do they develop a sense of spirituality that is inclusive of all children without proselytising them to the narrow confines of one denominational creed or belief?

What is interesting in our situation here at The Wyche is that we appear to have stumbled across a form of spirituality that we feel addresses those at both ends of the faith continuum. Whilst my deputy would not call himself an atheist I describe him, in words of the vernacular, as "our resident pagan." By his own admission he does not personally have a reference point for God and has not engaged with any form of spirituality in his own life either as a child or an adult. On the other hand both my parents held a deep Christian belief and I have been happy to continue in the faith of the family home. I lead one of the local churches and the Christian faith is an essential part of my everyday life. To this end we would appear to represent the two ends of the faith spectrum and yet the rest of this document seeks to set out how we developed a concept of spirituality that we both felt able to deliver throughout the school

What Spirituality isn't

As with most things in life it is sometimes easier to see what something is by first describing what it isn't and spirituality is a case in point. Many people come to the subject with such an immense amount of baggage that it is impossible to build anything of value on foundations that are not philosophically secure. Therefore let me state a little of the journey we have been on in dismantling the stumbling blocks on our journey to create a coherent spiritual curriculum. Much of the confusion relating to the subject often hinges upon semantics so sometimes simply clarifying terminology can break down barriers preventing clarity of thought.

Spirituality should not be confused with any of the following:

Religion: Spirituality has little to do with religion. As Clive Simpkins says *"Spirituality is not necessarily religious or even dependent on religion as its foundation"*. Religion is simply the formalised structure of a faith but as Jesus pointed out on more than one occasion, religion is often one of the biggest hindrances for those on a quest for true spirituality. (Matthew 23:1-10 provides one of many examples) Religion is man's attempt to seek links with the spiritual life through ritual, symbolism and metaphor. Whilst one can debate the merits of this approach the point most pertinent to our debate is to accept that religion is not necessarily synonymous with spirituality. It would be fair to say that the latter operates at a far deeper level than its religious counterpart. As David Hay states; *"religion tends to be associated with what is publicly available such as churches, mosques, bibles, prayer books, weddings and funerals"* and goes on to conclude that; *"an increasing number of people in Western countries want to distinguish it (spirituality) from religion"* In many ways they are right to do so and if we are to provide a clear focus for a spiritual curriculum we should ensure that we are developing in children a sense of spirituality rather than a sense of dry religiosity. As David Hay acknowledges most of us have negative associations with religion and yet *"Spirituality is almost always seen as much warmer, associated with love, inspiration, wholeness, depth, mystery and personal devotions like prayer and meditation"*

Religious Education: Religious education is principally an academic subject and is the study of theology and of comparative religions. All of this can be done in the mind and can bypass the heart and the soul entirely. We don't expect children who study elements of World War 2 in the History curriculum to imbibe Nazi philosophy. If we did we might think twice before teaching it but rather we accept that academic study fills the mind with information to be processed and learnt. The idea that RE lessons will deliver a spiritual curriculum in and of themselves is deeply flawed; it is academic study. Many who study theology at university would lay no claim to having a faith in God or any particular spiritual life at all. There is an important distinction that needs to be made between "knowing about God" and "knowing God".

Spirituality is not an Intelligence: For those conversant with Howard Gardner's theory on multiple intelligences you may be aware that he has sought to introduce further intelligences to the original framework proposed in 1983. However he stopped short of adding that of "Spiritual Intelligence". His rationale for this lay in the fact that his original work set out clear criteria for categorising intelligence and he found that the characteristics of spirituality did not lend themselves to being classed as a neurologically entity. There have been many that have challenged Gardner's thinking and have stated a case for what they have come to call SQ (Spiritual Quotient, relating it to the traditional IQ – Intelligence Quotient and latterly to Daniel Goleman's work on EQ – Emotional Quotient) but the point to draw from Gardner's work is his conclusion that spirituality is to be found somewhere other than the academic brain. Admittedly recent research, especially the work of Roux and Damasio, have shown the brain to be a storehouse for emotion as well as logical thought but Gardner's view remains that for those looking to cultivate spirituality it is best not thought of in terms of a rational intelligence but as something relating more to the heart and the soul.

Moral and Social: In its statement of aims the National Curriculum makes a clear distinction between the "Spiritual" and the "Moral and Social" elements. There is a danger that we treat spiritual development as synonymous with the moral teachings of the major religions. This has the propensity to reduce spirituality to a series of moral teachings. Many in education have been seduced by this notion. Nicholas Tate the Chief Executive of SCAA (School Curriculum Assessment Authority) stated at one point that *"although many can accept that truth in moral matters can be independent of God, the loss of the religious basis for morality has weakened its credibility"* His premise is that morality springs from a form of spirituality but sadly this is not necessarily the case. It is true that morality may spring out of a spiritual belief but it is not the essence of spirituality itself. As he himself later went on to say; it is possible to live a moral life totally devoid of any relationship with God. As David Hay rightly argues *"morality has its source at a deeper level than specific religious adherence, since it arises in the first place out of spiritual insight"* We should be careful not to meld morality and spirituality together treating them as synonymous as they each have a distinct and unique place in the life of mankind. For schools this means drawing a clear distinction between an assembly where the content is morally focused (not a bad thing I hasten to add) and one that is seeking to deliver a sense of spirituality. Once the distinction is clearly drawn it will prevent schools delivering assemblies that blur into an ill-conceived amorphous presentation of both.

Worship: Somewhat more controversially I would not necessarily equate the concept of worship with a school based definition of spirituality. The word "worship" comes from the Anglo-Saxon, *"weorthscipe,"* it means *"the act of focusing on that which is of greatest worth"* Within the Christian faith this clearly consists of proclaiming God as a deity of worth and traditionally the church has demonstrated this fact through songs, psalms and liturgy. The pre-cursor to any worship therefore is that there has to be something, or in a spiritual context usually someone, who is worthy of our worship. So whilst for the Christian, worship might seem to be a spiritual act flowing naturally out of their faith in God, for many children this will be an alien concept, especially if they have not formulated an opinion on whether God even exists. I am not saying that children should not be exposed to the patterns, ritual and songs of worship that a church, or a school assembly might offer, but spirituality is something deeper than the empty singing of words on the overhead projector. For instance how do we know how many of the congregation on Songs of Praise are worshipping or how many are agnostic and therefore simply singing? Again the footballer chosen to represent his country may choose as an act of discretion to sing or mouth the words of the national anthem even though he has clear republican and anti-monarchy views. The outward performance is not necessarily an indication of where the heart lies and it is the inner being which is the fount from which all true spirituality flows.

So... What on earth is Spirituality?

We initially used the two following definitions as a starting point to frame our discussions

Spirituality is that element of the human psyche that is concerned with the inner life. It transcends the mind, the heart and the emotions although we recognise that a spiritual experience may well impact on all of these.

A Spiritual Experience is one which opens the mind and the heart to a deeper understanding of oneself and one's place in the cosmos and the world.

However it was Jon (my deputy) who later came to summarise in one clear sentence the essence of what we were seeking to achieve when he said:

We touch spirituality when we encounter an experience on life's journey
that causes us to reflect on the deeper things of life,
its meaning and our purpose within it,
and as a consequence our lives are transformed.

Using this definition nearly all the staff concluded that there had been times in their own lives where they would claim to have had a spiritual experience. I remember vividly in one of the busiest and stressful times of my professional career sitting by a pond mesmerized by the water lilies floating on the surface. I was quite taken with the vibrant colours and fascinated by the intricate pattern of the petals. It was at that moment that I realised that there was more to life than SEF forms, performance targets, and impending Ofsted visits and deemed to be more pro-active in clawing my life back from the professional morass I had somehow allowed myself to be drawn into. For me it was a spiritual experience. Using our definition it was one of those times that caused me to reflect and put my life in greater perspective.

For Jon his visit to our link school in Tanzania was a spiritual and life changing experience. Such visits cause people to reflect on the wider world and the lives lived by others. This in turn acts as a mirror into one's own culture, causing us to re-evaluate our own beliefs, thoughts and values. I have taken many colleagues to Africa and they all come back changed as a result, because the experience is deeply spiritual.

In the Spring term of 2011 the Year 6 worked with a young man called Adam. Adam suffered from muscular dystrophy and was wheel chair bound. However he inspired the children amazing them with his artwork done painstakingly on the tray of his wheel chair. The following term Adam had passed away at the age of 28. Whilst all were aware that his life was time limited a deep sense of grief and disbelief followed, when the news came into school. It became evident that the children wanted to engage in the grieving process and the children expressed a wish to be present at the funeral. It was a time for adults and children to assess life afresh on so many levels. Looking back on the events of that term it became evident to both Jon and I that this event was immensely spiritual providing children with the opportunity to "reflect on the deeper things of life" although at that time we did not have the understanding of a spiritual framework to set it into.

As we journeyed in our thinking it became very apparent to all staff that everyday life is littered with opportunities to engage with a range of spiritual experiences that hitherto we may have discounted as simply being part of everyday life. The reception class' excitement at finding frost covered cobwebs one January morning, through to the Year 6 class viewing stinging nettles under the microscope, magnified enough to see the pipette shaped sac of poison that is injected upon the skin. Suddenly we began to see that these were not just opportunities to engage the mind in a Science lesson but in addition they became an occasion to engage the heart and soul in the wonder of creation thereby experiencing something on a spiritual as well as an academic level.

Viewed in this light the opportunities for spirituality seemed endless. What was interesting to note was that most of these were occurring outside of the traditional "assembly time". The school found itself aligning itself with the National Curriculum that stated that; *"All National Curriculum subjects provide opportunities to promote pupils' spiritual, moral, social and cultural development."* It is why our own school curriculum has, as one of its headings, *"Developing a sense of spirituality"* and it was always our intention that this would permeate the curriculum as a whole rather than being a daily bolt on activity when the whole school met together for twenty minutes in the hall.

It is the school's contention that in a world which is gathering pace in terms of the speed with which most of us live that if we can develop a generation of children who have learnt the importance of taking time out within a busy day to sit quietly and reflect on the deeper things in life we will have achieved much. So, just as reception children took time out to look at frost shapes and the Year 6 children took time to marvel at the wonder of stinging nettles my hope is that as these children become adults they will build similar times into their own personal lives. I can't help but think that all our lives would be enriched if we took time out of our day to refresh our souls with a period of deep reflection.

Hang on... Spirituality without God? That can't be right!

If this is your first reaction, then be heartened because it was mine too. The truth is that this could well be the response of both groups on either end of the faith continuum. Those who have a faith background might find it slightly incongruous to develop a spiritual framework without God whereas those of a more agnostic nature might feel that spirituality without any reference to the divine is not spirituality at all.

If we are to gain a full understanding of spiritual development in terms of a school setting then we will be required (as outlined earlier) to park the "religious" baggage that comes with the term. Whilst in churches spirituality will generally be thought of as a synonym for Christianity, in schools this is not the case. So whilst it may be true that all dogs are animals it does not mean that all animals are dogs. Certainly Christianity is a spiritual lifestyle but it does not mean that all spiritual lifestyles are Christian. There are many who worship a deity other than the Christian God but more importantly there are many who would claim to be spiritual but hold no religious conviction at all.

So should we dispense with God altogether in our spiritual thinking and how do we square that notion in a Church of England School?

Drawing faith into a Spiritual Curriculum

The spiritual curriculum we have explored so far allows for all children of all faiths, indeed those with none, to develop a greater understanding of themselves and their place in the world. This is a foundation and a starting point on which to build all spirituality, including that which relates to a particular faith.

I have likened the concept of spirituality as entering a room in which we can gain a sense of awe and wonder for ourselves and the world around us. However at one end of the room there should always be a door labelled "God" because if the experience we are trying to give children is truly spiritual in nature then it will always be possible to lead children into this additional experience. If you feel there is a disconnect between the two then the provision probably falls short of being spiritual.

Allow me to illustrate. When the reception children were reflecting on the frosted cobwebs and gaining a sense of life's perspective through nature, it would not be incongruous to ponder on God as a creator should one so wish. So too with the intricacy of the stinging nettle, there is a question which could be rightfully posed about whether it was created by chance or whether there is a divine mind behind creation? I appreciate that these examples maybe seem somewhat pointed and fall into the danger of subliminally inferring that there is a God. I also understand that some teachers may feel uncomfortable in presenting such an idea in this manner and we will address this later. But for now I am only seeking to establish that true spirituality should be inclusive in and of itself and yet it should also be readily able to graft a faith element into the experience.

The converse also illustrates this point. One may tell a moral tale which seeks to instil the principle that to love one another engenders a healthy sense of community. I frequently lead assemblies on such a theme but I accept that they are morally not spiritually based. It is harder to go through the "God" door from this starting point except to say something like "God would like it if you were nice to each other". There is no natural flow from one room into the other except the link between the moral concept and the endorsement of that lifestyle by a deity. Again we touch on the "Knowing God" and "Knowing about God" analogy noted earlier; except maybe this should be articulated as "Knowing what God likes" However one views it, we must accept that the former is spiritual whilst the latter is moral. It is vital that this distinction is clearly demarcated.

Interestingly enough if one turns the assembly theme on its head and allows children the opportunity to reflect on who loves them rather than who they should love, then it becomes easier to connect spiritually with God. Many children will undoubtedly be drawn to consider the love of their parents, their wider family and their friends but many others may have cause to ponder on the love God has for them as well.

Does there have to be the "God Bit?"

The question we posed ourselves as a staff was; *If the children are gaining a spiritual curriculum through the experiences outlined above do we always need to go through the extra door into the space set aside for a more traditional faith based spirituality?*

The answer is probably found in another question; *Why would you not want to?*

If schools are to "provide opportunities to promote pupils' **spiritual development**" (wording from the National Curriculum) then surely we should aim to provide as many opportunities in which children can develop their own personal faith should they wish. This must be done in a manner that is not didactic. Teachers should not state or even imply that God is the sole creator. This is not helpful in a school setting, however, giving children the opportunity to explore the question has to be an entitlement for every child and schools should not deny them this.

Rachael Heyhoe Flint captained the England ladies cricket team. When asked why she had taken up a sport traditionally dominated by men her answer was simple; one of her teachers put a cricket bat in her hand and as they say... the rest is history. Schools are here to broaden the horizons and perspectives of children in all areas of life not to narrow them. So, just as it is right for schools to give girls the opportunity to play cricket it is totally appropriate to provide opportunities for children to explore a faith based spirituality.

This might leave some staff in a position where they feel compromised expounding on faith and yet they might still have a desire not to short change children in this area of spiritual growth. Paul Finch, vicar of All Saints, the church upon which the school is founded, has been instrumental in working with teachers in this area. In an effort to allow teachers to share with integrity he has developed two approaches that the school has found immensely helpful.

Both relate to a concept he terms *"directive silence"*. At the heart of spirituality is the opportunity to reflect deeply into a given area of life and silence affords us this opportunity. However just as peace is not simply the absence of war so silence is not, in and of itself, a form of spirituality. The silence needs to be directed for the child. With this as a backdrop he then shared the following two strategies.

The first relates to posing questions rather than making statements. So with regards to the frosted cobwebs rather than stating; God made these, Paul has been encouraging the staff to just pose the question; *If you believe in God what do the cobwebs tell you about God?* The question links the moment with the divine for those who have a faith allowing them to reflect on a creator God. But within the same breath the teacher might want to continue to ask; and *if you don't believe in God, what do they tell you about the world we live in.* In general teachers felt more comfortable with this form of questioning.

The second approach Paul suggested was to soften any statements made in regards to God. In one assembly one of the teachers took the theme of "Those who help us". She gave some inspirational stories of people who with the odds stacked against them had achieved much through working together. At the end of the assembly she encouraged the children to ponder on those who have helped them. To set the scene she encouraged them with a "softer" faith based statement; *some people feel that God helps them when they are in trouble.* Whilst claiming no faith of her own she was simply stating something that is undoubtedly true, and can therefore be posed with no loss of integrity. Whilst I have no sympathy with the views of the Flat Earth Society I am happy to declare that there are some people who hold to the view that the earth is flat. In my own opinion they are woefully misguided but my integrity is not compromised by making the statement about them to others because it is true that some hold that particular opinion.

Both these approaches allow teachers to explore faith based spirituality without compromising their own beliefs but also both actively include those with a faith whilst not alienating those who, as yet, have not pursued any particular spiritual path.

Spirituality and the Curriculum

The point was made earlier that spirituality is not an academic subject and therefore there is an inherent challenge involved in embedding it into the curriculum. It should be readily apparent that a cognitive approach to the subject is wholly inappropriate and should be left to the RE lessons. So how do we plan for spirituality?

The first stage is to accept that spirituality cannot be boxed neatly into a lesson plan or a scheme of work. The most spiritual experiences in our curriculum are those that teachers tend to stumble across when, for instance, the frost falls on the cobwebs, or on a more sombre note when a friend of the school like Adam dies. This is why schools need to ensure they have a clear philosophical and pedagogical understanding regarding spiritual development. With this established, teachers will be able to take full advantage of opportunities as they arise using them to deepen children's spiritual understanding within a clear framework

However there is a place for planning but it is planning for experiences not for lessons. The national curriculum is right when it says that we should look for *"explicit opportunities to promote pupils' development in these areas"* it then goes on to list some of the curriculum subjects in which these might be explored, but the wording is correct, it is about providing "explicit opportunities" At present Paul Finch joins the staff at the beginning of each term and together we explore ways in which we can embed elements of spirituality into the taught curriculum.

For instance, the Year 2 class who were studying chocolate, decided to explore the life of John Cadbury, a remarkable man with a deep faith who developed a business plan centred on the well-being of his workers rather focusing on profit. The children discussed the ethos which drove him to establish something so radically different. They were then posed two questions; *what do you value in life?* and *how do we change our own lives?* Whilst it was obvious to the children that John Cadbury's faith was a central driving force they were also able to engage spiritually with the questions without drawing on the faith aspect if they so wished.

The Year 6 class looked at the Bloodhound team's attempt to break the land speed record in a vehicle designed to travel at 1,000mph. The children were encouraged to marvel at the design and the engineering but more importantly they focused on the driver and were posed the question; *what type of person would step into a car travelling at that speed knowing they were risking life and limb to achieve a particular goal?* This led on to the following question; *what is there in life that you are really passionate about?* Finally arriving at the time honoured question; *what would you be willing to die for?*

Through these and other examples it became evident that it was totally feasible to weave a sense of spirituality into topics we may have previously seen as solely academic. The Wyche Curriculum always had as one of its aims to *"develop a sense of spirituality"* and our fresh understanding has enabled us to provide a breadth of opportunities to explore this throughout the school day.

What we all acknowledged is that spirituality is experiential and therefore cannot be neatly packaged up into a standard unit plan. Furthermore it cannot be "taught" we can only create experiences for children that might lead to them into a sense of awe and wonder or a period of deep reflection. There needs to be an appreciation that the cognitive is about "filling the mind" whereas the experiential is about "opening the mind". They have different end points and therefore will require different journeys to get there.

As Thomas a Kempis once *said "For myself I would rather know what contrition feels like, than how to define it"* and this lies at the heart of the spiritual curriculum. In similar vein Rebecca Nye noted that *"Spirituality can be a powerful kind of knowing that is less worried about proving how you know"* In fact to engage with the *"how you know"* often detracts from the purity of the spiritual experience itself.

Concluding Remarks

In summary the spiritual experiences we provide should offer a base entitlement for all children. In the first instance they may make no explicit reference to God but there should always be the option of pursuing that path. Wherever possible we should endeavour to provide children with the opportunity to develop a faith based spirituality. If we claim that we want a breadth in the curriculum then it would be incongruous to narrow a child's spiritual development and deny them this opportunity. It is acknowledged that for some their spirituality development will focus on themselves and their place in the wider world whilst for others it will increasingly provide the opportunity to develop an ever deepening personal faith.

Postscript

Lest this article gives the impression that every child in the school is spiritually developing at an exponential rate let me shatter your illusions with the following true story. A boy turned to his teaching assistant whilst the new signage for the school was being put in place and asked *"So why are we The Wyche Coffee School?"*

R FONICS SUE-PURR-FLEW-US?

Wot! No Phonics?

It would seem that any school that dares to question the validity of synthetic phonics these days is in danger of being burnt at the educational stake as a complete heretic. So whilst I would obviously hold to the view that phonics have a role to play in the teaching of spelling I am not fully buying into the notion that they are the pot of gold at the end of the Literacy Rainbow that will solve all our spelling ills.

The current obsession with synthetic phonics was somewhat cemented into the psyche of all teachers through the "Letters and Sounds" document presented to the government by Jim Rose and rolled out into all schools in 2006. The document had much to commend it but it emphasised only one approach. It also stated that phonics, should be taught daily *"at least up until the end of year 2"* As I say I have no problem with teaching phonics but I do have grave reservations about teaching them into Year 2 for the majority of children.

In my opinion there comes a point at which teaching discrete phonics becomes superfluous; time to light the stake we spoke of earlier! Having observed various phonics lessons it is evident that once a child has reached a point where he recognises that the bird's beak may be spelt; "beak", "beek" or "beke" the role of "teaching" phonics has reached a natural conclusion. The child does not require further teaching on phonics but needs to learn which one of these spellings (all of which are potentially phonetically correct) is appropriate in the context in which it is being used.

I appreciate that the teaching up until this point will probably have been based mainly around skills acquisition and taught through discrete phonics lessons with little attempt to contextualise the learning. However this strategy is no longer appropriate for the teaching of spelling in a post-phonic phase. At this point the emphasis switches from skills acquisition to skill application and this should be explored in the arena of text based learning. The only way for the child to realise that a bird has a "beak" and not a "beek" is to root their understanding in the context of written text.

There is a danger with sustaining the teaching of phonics too long. The truth is that if the child already knows how to "spell" the word phonetically then they are simply struggling to draw on the correct version within a particular context. Without this particular skill set we may end up with phonetically correct spellers who write the following poem:

Spell chequer
By Jerrold H. Zar

Eye have a spelling chequer,
It came with my Pea Sea.
It plane lee marks four my revue
Miss Steaks I can knot sea.

Eye strike the quays and type a whirred
And weight four it two say
Weather eye am write oar wrong
It tells me straight a weigh.

Eye ran this poem threw it,
Your shore real glad two no.
Its vary polished in its weigh.
My chequer tolled me sew.

A chequer is a bless thing,
It freeze yew lodes of thyme.
It helps me right all stiles of righting,
And aides me when eye rime.

Each frays come posed up on my screen
Eye trussed too bee a joule.
The chequer pours o'er every word
Two cheque sum spelling rule.

This poem wonderfully illustrates that it is only the context that can establish errors in spelling. You will also observe that the reason why the spell checker cannot pick them up is because it checks words in isolation and therefore outside of any context. There is always the risk that the teaching of spelling through discrete lessons using words out of context will simply replicate the same mistake.

Related to this is the oft quoted fact that English is one of the most complex languages in the world to learn. English is not a phonetic language. By contrast Swahili is totally phonetically based, reading an unknown word is relatively straight forward as the word is pronounced as it is written. So "Jambo" (meaning Hallo) is pronounced just as you might expect. In English why should "cough" be pronounced "cof" and yet "bough" be pronounced "bow" – or should that be "bow", as in rhyming with "low"! George Bernard Shaw was once asked to pronounce the word "Ghoti." He replied "Fish" and when asked why he explained it as follows: the gh = f as in rough; the o = i as in women; the ti = sh as in nation.

It is not possible to "teach" these aspects of spelling divorced from a meaningful context. So although "bough" rhymes with "cow", "cough" rhymes with "off" and "rough" rhymes with "puff", it is also true that "though" rhymes with "Joe" and "through" rhymes with "too". The same applies with the frequent use of homophones in the English language with words such as sea and see; for and four; or hear and here.

The traditional approach (which sadly many schools are returning to due to the renewed emphasis on phonics as well as the arrival of SPAG) hinges on the principle of teaching spelling in dedicated lessons outside of the context of the child's own writing. Often the focus is on teaching phonic patterns and spelling rules. The evidence is overwhelming that this form of de-contextualised learning is flawed. At best it renders little impact on children's spelling within their written work and at worse can have a detrimental effect on the progress of proficient spellers. In 1973 two researchers, Simon and Simon, programmed computers with 200 spelling rules and then gave the same computer 17,009 words to spell, it failed in over half. Indeed when 10 year old children were tested on the words they outscored the computer.

More recent research from Victoria University, Wellington demonstrates a further danger in this teaching approach. Their study sought to compare children taught with explicit phonics and those taught through a more text-centred approach. The results showed that even with a high level of dependence on phonics the use of sounding out in Year 1 children made very little difference to their overall word accuracy in reading text. More alarmingly was the fact that the children taught through a whole text approach were able to read much faster and with greater accuracy. They were also able to read words with irregular spellings more effectively than their phonic taught peers. Interestingly these disparities continue over time so that Scottish University students taught exclusively on phonics as children were worse at reading new or unfamiliar words that did not follow regular taught letter sounds than those taught through holistic written texts.

Suffice to say, learning is not about the compartmentalisation and storing of separate fragments of knowledge. The brain is a unified whole and understanding is developed as the mind makes connections on a variety of levels through active engagement with new material. Using a slightly related example, when a child says to you "What does irascible mean?" it is incredibly difficult to construct an answer that takes in the full orb of the meaning of the word. Whilst it is true it means grumpy, it is more than that, as it relates more to someone being irritable as well as snappy, although all these words don't quite get to the true meaning. How much easier when a person displays this characteristic to simply say "He is irascible." The reason is that the latter creates a multi-dimensional explanation allowing the brain to instantly make a high level of multiple connections which greatly assist true understanding. The arbitrariness of a "word shrapnel" approach is very flat and 2-dimensional in comparison. All learning should take place in the richest and broadest of environments and the teaching of spelling is no different. So to assume that "teaching" children pockets of knowledge in isolation away from real texts will allow them to make progress is defective pedagogy.

The overly structured emphasis in teaching is a response not just to national governmental initiatives but often a pedagogical reaction to the "osmosis" approach that proliferated previously. To caricature it slightly it hinged around whether spelling should be "caught or taught" and many came to believe that simply exposing children to a range of texts would enhance their spelling. Of course (as with many aspects of pedagogy) there is an element of truth in this but there is a fundamental weakness within the thinking. Let me illustrate with the following passage of text:

Rome is accessed from the sea through the port of Civitavecchia which lies 80 km North West of the Italian capital on the shores of the Tyrrhenian Sea, which in turn is part of the Mediterranean Sea.

Bearing in mind you have only just read the passage see if you can name (without referring back to the text) the port that Rome accesses for its goods and services. The chances are that whilst you will have read the whole sentence our mind tends to gloss over words we don't need to "read" to maintain the basic meaning of the text. If we don't even "read" the text what chance do we stand of being able to spell the word. Without looking back at the text how well would you be able to spell either the port or the sea on which it sits? How many of us can spell the word "Mediterranean" without resorting to pen and paper to gain a visual version with which we can check accuracy? Whilst it could be argued that it was the first time you may have seen the first of the two words, how many times have you seen and read the word "Mediterranean" and yet still the majority of adults struggle to spell it correctly.

The flaw in the "Spelling is caught" argument is that we "read for meaning" not to assist our spelling. If we can make sense of the text then we feel no particular compulsion to engage with the text at a deeper level – indeed why should we? Using another example; the majority of people read this infamous phrase (right) as "Paris in the Spring." This might explain why some learned academics that are very well read do not excel in the area of spelling. The truth is that secure spellers are those who notice the patterns and forms in individual

words rather than those who are well read. This simply illustrates Peters point that *"Reading alone does not determine whether a child will be good at spelling." (Peters, 1985)* So it is not too surprising to find that research has shown that contrary to popular opinion it is often the fastest readers who make the weakest spellers due to their inability to focus in on the structure of individual words and letter patterns within them.

Keys to a Successful Spelling Programme

If one takes all the research into consideration I would say there are several key areas to be addressed in developing a cogent spelling programme.

(i) Phonics

It is evident that whilst some children will bypass the phonics hurdle on their way to mastering reading for others it is a key foundational block on that journey. I don't advocate not teaching phonics that would be foolhardy but I would suggest that short sharp lessons, often no longer than ten to fifteen minutes will allow children to make good progress in the Early Years. Some children at The Wyche maintain phonics teaching into Year 1 but by no means all and by Year 2 phonics remains the sole domain of those on the SEN register. This is not a principle based on our particular catchment because historically we used to teach phonics well into Year 2.

Rather it is founded on the belief, as stated earlier, that once a child can "spell" phonetically then they should quickly move onto contextualised learning through their own written work at the earliest opportunity.

(ii) "Invented" or "Emergent" Spelling

The use of "invented spelling" promoted by the National Writing Project in the 1980's has now become mainstream thinking and was introduced to *"separate the specific problem of learning to spell from the other more satisfying matter of getting on with writing" (Smith)*. It enables children to engage in the creativity of the writing process leaving the secretarial aspects to be addressed through the re-drafting process. Whilst the main focus may have been to promote creativity, the philosophy has been proven to have had a positive impact on spelling. Research has shown that children taught in this manner have a greater grasp of spelling strategies. This is due to the fact that, in writing their own spellings they are actively engaging themselves with letter patterns and phonetic sounds. Whilst the phrase "flying sorser" is not correct it compels children to look at how words might be constructed and encourages them to engage in, (what experts call) "phono-grampheme divergence" or the turning of sounds into written form. In addition it also provides a powerful diagnostic tool for the teacher. In this particular case it is clear that the child has a clear understanding of the sounds "or" and "s" but has not seen that "au" can make a sound comparable to "or" and that words can use the soft "c" to create an "s" sound. Wherever possible this "emergent" approach to spelling should be encouraged with the one important caveat that whilst we... *"should recognise worthy attempts made by children to spell words we should also correct them selectively and sensitively. If this is not done, invented spelling could become ingrained" (Letters and Sounds p13)*

(iii) Understanding

The key to progressing in spelling is to discern the patterns that underpin the English language. So whilst we might acknowledge that the words "Clodamation" and "grhyaikht" are both nonsense words, neither of which appear in any English dictionary, we would however, readily appreciate that the former follows linguistic conventions more closely than the latter. It is this ability to imbibe these patterns which allows proficient spellers to make good progress. Whilst pondering on this I watched my wife seek to complete a crossword over the holidays. The thought processes she undertook to solve the clue showed a clear understanding of spelling pattern. Suppose one came to a word that had the clue " a type of cream" and you knew from the rest of the crossword that the solution had the letters; c _ _ _ t _ d. You might surmise that the letter after the "c" might be an "l" or an "r", of course you would know it would not be a "d" or an "f". You might be aware that it could also possibly be a vowel, which it may well be. You could also deduce that there was a strong possibility that the letter preceding the final "d" might be an "e". Then starting with a blend one would need a vowel and then maybe a double consonant, making the word "clotted". Such a thought process shows a clear understanding of the syntax of morphemes and graphemes in individual words. As Gibson and Levin stated *"spelling is a kind of grammar for letter sequences that generates permissible combinations without regard to sound" (Gibson and Levin)* This is where we need to take children; they need to develop a deep and secure understanding of the principles that govern the structure of words.

The danger is that we resort back to traditional grammar lessons to teach these principles but that is not a cogent way forward. The wording of the National Literacy Strategy document was clear in this regard. It stated unequivocally that children should "explore" the patterns in words for themselves and should *"identify mis-spelt words in their own writing; to keep individual lists and learn how to spell them" (NLS document 1998)* The use of individual spelling logs is instrumental in this. Once again the wording of the NLS guides the thinking that should underpin this. It stated that... *pupils should explore the full range of spelling conventions and rules outlined within the strategy, e.g. What happens to words ending in "f" when a suffix is added?* It was clear that they believed an individual child should collate their own spellings looking for patterns and rules that enabled their future spelling to become more secure.

An emphasis on visual learning

Somewhat related to the aspect above is the fact that sight is the preferred sense for the human race. So although our teaching should maintain an obvious multi-sensory approach there should be a weighted emphasis towards the visual as the principal learning approach. Most of us, if not all of us, have a preference to "see" whether spellings are correct. How many of us as adults, once we have spelt out a word in our head have to write it down to "see" if it is right.

The strategy of correcting spelling by copying out individual words undertaken in many classes would appear in the first instance to have a modicum of wisdom to it. However, research shows that children tend to resort to copying letter by letter thereby removing the visual patterning element required for successful learning. This is similar to our use of the telephone directory where we look up a telephone number, dial the individual digits and mentally wipe out the number so effectively that if we were given the wrong number by the person at the other end of the phone we would no doubt have to look up the number again. It is the patterning that is vital. Although we may forget the 11 digit phone number we might remember these 11 digits easier 0,2,4,6,8,10,12,14 it is the pattern that unlocks the understanding. So too with letters we may struggle to remember the sequence; *l,r,a,m,a,e,t,n,i,p* but if we order them differently; "p,a,r,l,i,a,m,e,n,t somehow they become easier to take on board. The Look-Cover-Write-Check method was an attempt to address this problem and encouraged children to memorise the word as a whole rather than breaking it down into its individual constituent letters. It remains a secure, tried and tested technique and is preferable to an individual letter copying approach.

The Assessment of Spelling

The traditional approach of the weekly spelling test is held by many as sacrosanct and remains a key feature in the majority of schools. Its limitations are obvious to all, in the sense that, teachers readily accept that a child may be able to remember a series of spellings over a weekend for a test on Monday but the reality is that the test is more related to "Short term memory retention" than an activity strategically focused on the principles of spelling. This has been further confirmed recently by MRI scans which have shown that when children learn spellings for a test they are using a different part of their brain entirely from when they tackle spellings in the context of their own writing. (Brian Male, address given at The Curriculum Foundation, 26th April 2010) If spelling tests are to remain a feature of school life they need to heed Jim Rose's advice that they should be rooted in a broad and rich Literacy curriculum. To this end the "learning" of high frequency words which children have the opportunity to use readily in the context of their own work is seemingly philosophically cogent. One might also argue that the consolidation of phonetic sounds learnt that week is similarly of benefit. However the use of random spelling lists for children to learn weekly will be marginally beneficial at best.

Conclusion

Many would feel there is a debate to be had about the importance of spelling in this increasingly informal world where the text messaging generation appears to drive a wedge between their own unique form of communication and what many call "standard English". This article has sidestepped that debate, not because the school believes it does not have some merit, for if writing is about communicating meaning then it is probable that such a debate has a great deal of validity, but my vision for the school is broader and wider than the single issue of how words are spelt. I would wish that children at The Wyche would leave with a fascination with words and their structure. My hope is that they will have a natural interest to explore how words originate and how they develop as societies shift and change through time. These elements of learning transcend completely the notion that a school's only mandate is to produce "good spellers". Instead we should be leaving children with something much richer – an enquiring mind and an appreciation of the richness of their native language.

THE BEGUILING MYTH OF
CHILD INITIATED LEARNING

Introduction

If I was asked to express my own educational philosophy I would describe myself as Child Centric, Emergent and Constructivist. Constructivist[4], in the sense that I believe the richest learning is encountered when children are enabled to engage their own thinking and develop their own constructs in exploring any concept. As Vygotsky and Bruner point out this is not random exploration but a process that is constructed with direct "scaffolding" from the teacher, who guides the children towards a full grasping of the principle to be learnt. Emergent, in the sense that this understanding "emerges" from within the child and "Child Centric" because the ultimate motivation for any piece of learning should come from

---

[4] Constructivism is rooted in the belief that children need to "construct" learning for themselves. It does not hold to the view that the teacher is the fount of all knowledge and the pupil an empty vessel into which knowledge should be poured. Instead it sees that the child brings to the classroom their own experience of life and that they are therefore able to make sense of learning for themselves. In this scenario the role of the teacher is not to be *the sage on the stage* but instead they need to become *the guide on the side* scaffolding the child towards a position where they can develop their cognitive constructs in a given area of academic learning.

the child who has been empowered to learn for themselves and can therefore engage actively with the task. It will surprise no-one therefore that when my Reception teacher informed me that she wanted to develop a "Child Initiated Curriculum" I was fully supportive of such a venture.

Elly Harrison, who teaches a mixed Reception and Year 1 class here at The Wyche, wanted to push the boundaries of the Child Centric concept to see how far one could develop a curriculum that originated and was driven solely by the children. So she developed a system where the children would select the topic to be covered; they would then pose questions that they wanted to explore and then propose activities they wanted to undertake throughout the term. The advantages of this approach compared with the more traditional teacher led curriculum are obvious but are still worth articulating.

The children had a huge "buy in factor" with the topic subject they had chosen with ideas as diverse as Space, Pets, The Seaside and Pirates.
Their ability to pose their own questions for study built on this further. So not only were they able to choose the topic but they were also empowered to select the aspects to be covered. So in studying the Pirates the children wanted to know; "How do their ships move?" and also "What do they eat and where do they get their food from?"

The questions also acted as a powerful assessment tool and these drove the curriculum accordingly. The child whose question "How does light get into the eye?" showed the teacher that they were working at a level well beyond the expected norm of a Foundation Stage child and this allows for the curriculum to be tailored appropriately for their needs especially for the more able who have the opportunity to show their true ability

They were then encouraged to develop learning activities that would answer some of the questions they had posed. This allowed the children to see themselves as an instrumental part of the learning process as they became the "learner" rather than a child to whom the curriculum was passively done unto. They would design experiments to test hypotheses and create activities that enabled them to explore the areas of learning they themselves had first set up through their questions.

The power of this approach should not be underestimated as it establishes a powerful cultural message at the onset of a child's school life that they are a learner and that they are a key player within that learning journey. The children come to see education as a joint enterprise between teacher and pupil rather than a didactic one way flow of information and facts that they passively need to imbibe.
The whole process is "emergent" and starts with the learning coming from the child, a position which I would naturally fully endorse and sits very comfortably within my "constructivist" pedagogy.

The visit of the OFSTED team in 2009 simply sought to underscore the excellence of this approach. The report stated;

"Excellent teaching and an exciting curriculum help children to make exceptionally good progress. Children are responsible for planning their own curriculum and devising questions they would like to be answered. This innovative approach towards learning engages their interest fully and develops their confidence and self-esteem extremely well. As a result, children cooperate extremely well, are very independent and learn how to make sensible choices. During the inspection, children were particularly enjoying finding out about sinking and floating as part of a topic about pirates. They managed this work for themselves very sensibly, identifying which stage of the activity they were involved in"

So far so good but...

The Challenge of the Black Swan

In 16th Century Britain there was an expression in common use which stated that "a good person is as rare as a black swan" It was a Latin phrase based on the understanding at that time that there was no such thing as a black swan. It was a thought fashioned on the views of Aristotle who used the white swan as a known possibility in deductive reasoning but the Black Swan as being highly improbable. The reality is that until the New World was explored in the 17th century the perceived wisdom was that all swans were white. When explorers returned from Australia claiming that the Black Swan actually existed, it obviously challenged the notion that all swans were white.

In 2007 Nassim Nicholas Taleb published a book entitled the Black Swan - The Impact of the Highly Improbable. Far from being a book on wildlife in the Australian outback Taleb sought to use this antipodean animal as an analogy to demonstrate the fragility of any system of thought. He stated that any set of conclusions quickly unravel once any of its fundamental claims are disproved. So it was that the discovery of the Black Swan was the undoing of the infamous phrase undermining its basic tenet completely.

The power of Taleb's use of the swan as a simile of understanding, demonstrates clearly that everything we hold as true is based on what we think we know. However the more profound thought comes from pondering the flip side of this argument, namely that what is probably more important is the realisation that; we don't know what we don't know.

What has this got to do with Child Initiated Learning?

As I observed the children taking control of their own learning I was singularly impressed by its child centric nature but I began to see the principle of "You don't know what you don't know" being played out in the planning process which lay at the heart of the Early Years curriculum in the school.

Henry Ford, a pioneering of the burgeoning car industry in the early 20th century once said *"If I had asked people what they had wanted they would have said a faster horse"* What he was demonstrating in this comment is the Black Swan principle, namely that seeing as people did not know that a car could exist they worked within their own paradigm of consciousness and therefore considered that the only panacea (from within their own understanding) had to be the improvement of the transport they knew at the time.

The same is true of children and their learning. Whilst it is commendable to engage the children in all areas and levels of curriculum planning there has to come a point where the child initiated approach hits a cul-de-sac and children enter the territory of not knowing what they don't know.

Aware that a study of the Mayan tribe is part of the KS2 History curriculum I decided to explore the self-initiated planning approach myself, as an adult. It is not a historical culture I am particularly well aquainted with and interestingly the same cul-de-sac operated for me as it does for the children. Conscious that the tribe were South American I wondered what they might wear given their hot climate, I also wanted to know what they might eat. My knowledge of other historical tribes caused me to question who their enemies were and what religious system underpinned their cultural and social lives. However I never thought to ask the question "Why is the Mayan calendar based on a 260 day cycle and how does it dovetail into the more conventional 365 day calendar of the rest of the world" Why? For the simple reason that I didn't know they had such a calendar and therefore I didn't know what I didn't know.

This revelation caused me to reflect on our own practice in the Foundation Stage. In truth Elly was already drawing similar conclusions from a more practical rather than philosophical standpoint. Her thoughts centred on the fact that if the curriculum is a statutory entitlement for all children, and the children don't come up with any questions or activities related to any given subject then where does that leave the school in terms of curriculum coverage? It was evident even in its early stages that the child initiated approach needed to be supplemented by some area of teacher driven learning and in truth it has been from its inception.

The deeper question that we both sought to address however, related to our desire to marry up our wish to deliver a child centric curriculum with as little compromise as possible in terms of teacher direction. It was with this in mind that we started to explore a fresh approach that would build on (not dismantle) the current excellent practice that existed already within the Foundation Stage Curriculum in the school.

Springboards for Learning

The key to moving forward in any area is to articulate clearly where you are in the present. For us it was simple, the children had ownership of the topic chosen, they had ownership of the questions they posed but they were limited by what they knew. The limitations centred on their own experience of life, which at four years old is not extensive, but also on the principle of the Black Swan and the elements which they don't know. In addition to this there was a time frame issue for children of this age. Whilst it was true that they had designed the topic and the questions these were done either at the beginning of the term or in the latter weeks of the previous term. So sometimes the topic chosen in July was still being completed in December. Life moves on quite fast in a young child's life and issues of relevance started to come to the fore as we questioned whether the topic questions were still driving the children forward in their learning. In similar vein it was noted that the questions they had posed at the beginning may not be the same as the ones they might have had half way through and definitely might not be the ones they had towards the end. With this in mind we came up with the concept of "Springboard" activities.

The Springboard activities occur regularly through the topic and are designed to run alongside the learning of the children allowing the questioning and exploring to deepen as the topic runs, helping to combat the "what we don't know" issue.

For example the children undertook a study of the seaside in the summer term. Their early questions revolved around ones you might expect from a class of Foundation Stage children and provided a good initial starting point for the teacher to develop a secure curriculum framework. The topic included a trip to the seaside which occurred half way through the topic. It was at this point that one could see the Black Swan principle kicking in.

At the start of the topic none of the children asked; *why are there donkey rides on the beach?* nor did they enquire as to; *why the theatre was on the pier?* This was for the simple reason that until they had visited the resort they had no understanding that there were donkeys on the beach or that the pier had a theatre. These two questions, one looking at the traditions of a seaside town and the other looking at entertainment in Victorian times have the ability to engage the children at a deeper level but the important thing to note is that they are drawn out by constricting the Black Swan principle and broadening the understanding of what children know by bringing fresh knowledge into the realm of their experience.

It became apparent from this that the child centred approach can only thrive in an arena where the Black Swan principle is significantly reduced. The limitations of what we know hinder our ability to develop questioning skills at a deep level. So on the back of this we developed the Springboard activities. As before the children chose the topic and posed a range of questions at the outset but then throughout the topic there would be experiences built in which would broaden the understanding of children and allow them to re-engage with the questioning process at a deeper level. It is one thing to say at the beginning of a topic; *what does a hamster drink?* but when the animal is in the class the children might notice how regularly they drink and pose the deeper question of; *how much water do they drink in a day?* or alternatively; *does the hamster drink more water at night or in the day?* The experiential activity of hosting the hamster reduces the Black Swan principle, enriches the knowledge of the children thereby driving the questions deeper.

This would not have to be a one off process but could develop into a spiral curriculum where the questions continue to be refined and continue to develop in depth. At present we have a Bearded Dragon in school so the children might wish to compare how much water he drinks and explore reasons why one animal drinks more than the other. This might lead on to further questions but the emphasis is always on increasing and broadening the experience so that the questioning gets deeper.

The springboard activities seek to promote this spiral element to the curriculum. So whilst at the beginning of a Geography unit the children may well ask; What is Australia like? After someone has come to answer their initial questions the children they will then be afforded the opportunity to engage afresh with the questioning process at a deeper level. The visiting speaker therefore acts as a springboard upon which the next set of questions can be drawn. This is founded on the belief that the richest learning experiences are enhanced through depth not just breadth. As those working with more able pupils will readily recognize, a key factor in differentiating work is not just to give them more of the same, nor just to take the concepts on further but rather to increase the complexity of any given task which in turn will enrich the questioning and drive the understanding deeper.

WOULD IT BE KINDER TO HAVE SEAL PUT DOWN?

Analysis: Testing the Emotions

I have never been particularly good at the "doing nothing" type of thing, so whilst I was on holiday this summer and soaking up some Mediterranean sun I decided to fill the time listening to some of the podcasts from the BBC. I stumbled across a programme in the Analysis series entitled: Testing the Emotions which was first broadcast on 7th March 2011. The information on the programme stated that "Fran Abrams asks whether children need to be taught emotional and social skills in school". I listened with interest.

In one of the opening sentences the presenter proudly declared that "On this week's Analysis we are going to be going off our core curriculum" Bearing in mind that I consider the social and emotional aspects of school to be its core curriculum I could feel myself cleaving away from the thesis of the programme before it had hardly started. To emphasise the topic's importance the programme drew on aspects of research, such as the UNICEF league table for well-being where the UK languishes in bottom place. It then turned its focus onto one particular school; Bournemouth Park, Primary School in Southend, to exemplify quality practice in the teaching of social skills. I appreciate that for the sake of journalistic effect and the engagement of their listeners the programme needed to trawl the country to find the most avant-garde form of practice and so they focused on one particular workshop. Here the children were being taught that they all had seven energy centres residing in their bodies and that these are all different colours. The presenter referred to it rather disparagingly as "a new age philosophy" and to be fair even the Headteacher admitted that she "... wouldn't say she whole heartedly believed in it". However she was very articulate in her belief that social and emotional intelligence lay at the heart of a child's development and of course this is something with which I would greatly concur.

Despite the emphasis on the programme being on the social and emotional development of the children, like most educational offerings in the media, the subject quickly regressed to the well-worn theme of "raising standards" and of course the raising of standards in the academic sphere. Research was wheeled out that showed that social programmes raised attainment by 1%. As the presenter pointed out Roger Weissberg's research claimed that such teaching raised achievement by 11% but as was pointed out, whilst his study was drawn from 200 schools the results used for the final percentage came from a sub group of 35 schools with many of these having corresponding academic learning programmes attached to them. The programme ended with a concluding summary that ran something like; social and emotional programmes are simply warm and fuzzy additions to the curriculum that appear to add very little to the academic progress of the child.

The programme caused me to reflect on two areas in this regard: Firstly, why are we still so obsessed with the fact that the only true measure of a school's worth is its output in academic terms especially when research shows that it is the "soft skills" which employers are crying out for? The second was the "teaching" of social and emotional skills and whether we should be using programmes such as SEAL (Social and Emotional Aspects of Learning) to deliver these elements of the curriculum.

The Academic Obsession

We have become totally preoccupied with the academic output of schools to the extent that we view the success of any educational programme through this lens. If the SEAL programme or the workshop of seven colours does not lead to a consequent rise in attainment in the subjects politicians deem to be of utmost importance, (notably English and Maths) then they are deemed to be at best a luxury in terms of curriculum time that few schools can afford and at worse a total failure, to be quickly written off as a complete waste of time.

But surely we should be teaching social and emotional skills to enhance the social and emotional elements of a child's life and well-being. There is an obvious flaw in the logic of those who claim that these lessons should be withdrawn from the curriculum because they don't enhance skills in Literacy or Mathematics. By the same token we could remove Music because it doesn't enhance French, in fact why not replace Maths because it doesn't raise standards in Literacy. The truth is we don't teach Maths to improve Literacy we teach Literacy for that, we teach Maths to improve Maths. So too with the social and emotional curriculum, we teach it because we want children to spend their time in school as well-rounded and socially-adjusted individuals enjoying the company of others and developing an increasing depth of relationships with the adults and their peers in the school community.

The narrow academic view of education is something that belongs to another century. It had its day in the Victorian era when knowledge was everything and those who succeeded in life tended to be those who excelled in the curriculum of the day which was heavily academically focused. What we often fail to appreciate is that for centuries prior to that unique time period that followed the industrial revolution, education was viewed as an activity as much of the heart as it was of the brain. From Aristotle in the 4th century BC who said "Educating the mind without educating the heart is no education at all" through to the 19th Century when Thomas More the poet and Philosopher said "I'd like to see us educate the soul and not just the mind" It was believed that the place of education was to enlighten mankind not simply to fill the mind in a manner that would allow students to regurgitate it all sitting in single desks in a school hall in June. I do believe that much of what we deem to be good education today would be totally unrecognisable if those from past generations visited our schools today.

However it is not the past to which we should be looking. There is an increasingly welter of evidence to show that it is those with strong emotional skills that are best prepared for life both within school and in their adult life. As Eisner (2004) once said "The goal of school is not to do well in school but to do well in life" The APPG report (April 2014) revealed that there is a contingent within our own government who increasingly feel we should return to a form of education that educates the heart as well as the mind. They wrote "When we talk about education in this country our first thoughts turn exclusively to exam results and academic achievement... if our education system focused on the "soft skills", young people would leave school better equipped to face life and its challenges" A year earlier the Cabinet Office expressed similar thoughts; "Non cognitive skills are increasingly considered to be as important as – or even more important than cognitive skills or IQ in determining academic and employment outcomes" (The Impact of non-cognitive skills, Cabinet Office 2013). So too The Social Mobility Commission Report (2013) that said; "Schools need to focus on developing Character Skills alongside improving their pupil's academic attainment. It is not a question of either/or. Schools need to be doing both" The CBI report published in 2014 continued this theme. Rob Wall, CBI head of education and employment policy, said: "The CBI had found 89% of British firms had regarded attitudes to work and character as the most important factor when recruiting graduates."

The truth is we have moved on from the "Industrial Revolution" and find ourselves in the "Technological Revolution" where a new set of skills are needed. All research and all calls from industry are for a workforce that is interpersonally strong and therefore these skills should lie at the heart of a nation's core curriculum. It is interesting to note that in Singapore, a country held up as being a model of excellence by the DfE in their report "The Importance of Teaching", have made a paradigm shift in their own curriculum. Heng Swee, the education minister told delegates at their national conference that; "Values and character development must form the core of our education" (Ministry of Education seminar 2011). The Australian National Curriculum also includes the following sentence in one of its opening paragraphs; "Education is as much about building character as it is about equipping students with specific skills" (National Framework for Values education p2). The point is that these countries have moved on from what Chris Shute (1998) called the "ceaseless quest for a better way to stuff information into children" and instead are seeking to develop the whole child into an emotionally mature individual who will be well equipped to contribute to their society in the 21st century.

It is time therefore to stop viewing children as if they are "Brains on legs" and start to see that raising children's self-esteem, enriching their soul and developing their interpersonal skills and relationships with others should lie at the heart of education not on its periphery. Traditionally these skills have been categorised in what many have termed "the hidden curriculum" but why would we want to hide them? Let's bring them to the fore as other countries have and declare that these are the skills children will need in their adult life and where better to learn them than in the highly pastoral environment of a primary classroom.

Can Social and Emotional Skills be taught?

As much as I am passionate about our education system being built around a core curriculum of social and emotional skills alongside the more traditional academic subjects I have always been somewhat sceptical of some of the approaches suggested in the delivering of them.

In the early part of my teaching career the discrete teaching of PSHE, as it was then called, did not appear on the curriculum. However by the mid 1990's educationalists had started to discuss how it should be taught. In more recent years the government introduced the SEAL (Social and Emotional Aspects of Learning) programme which came in on the back of the SEL (Social Emotional Learning) programme from the United States that was being heralded at the time as an unqualified success. So two years after its initial roll out in 2005 the SEAL programme was being used in 90% of primary schools and 70% of secondary schools.

For myself I have always been somewhat resistant to teaching the social elements of the curriculum in the form of a programme or even, to a certain extent, in the form of planned and structured lessons. The debate hinges around the well-worn question: Can social and emotional skills be taught? Educationalists stand on either side of the fence but I would contend they are asking the wrong question. The focus for most people is upon lessons, short or medium term planning etc. but I would suggest they are starting from the wrong end of the debate. These are the micro elements, or the small details of curricular implementation. To look at this debate in context we need to be asking questions on the macro level and therefore the correct starting point would turn the question on its head and ask: What are schools for?

Schools by definition are social and emotional arenas within themselves. They have to be because they involve people. For the child entering school their first class becomes their social learning arena. It is here that they learn to share toys in the role play area, listen to the teacher and value the views and opinions of others. Those teaching early years seem to accept this as a key aspect of their role. It should be no surprise therefore that when the government put out the "Call for Review of EYFS" in 2011 81% of respondents said support for personal, social and emotional development was the most important thing settings could do to support a child's learning and development. But the interesting aspect is the simple fact that reception teachers have undertaken all this without having to resort to formal lessons, organised programmes, or medium term plans. They have long recognised that social and emotional issues are best taught in context. The best time to discuss "relational conflict" is not in a lesson pre-planned on a Friday afternoon (although there may be a place for this, but somehow I doubt it) but shortly after the fight over the tractor on the farm play mat. Because schools contain people, and people come with relational issues then there will be plenty of opportunities for people to develop their social and emotional intelligence within this setting. The astute amongst you will note that I use the term "people" not "children" because it will not have escaped the attention of any of us that there are ample opportunities for staff to develop and hone their social and emotional skills in the context of the staffroom as much as children are able to refine theirs in the context of the classroom!

So how do we learn social and emotional skills? We learn them by simply being with people and living life alongside them. Just as when objects draw alongside each other in the natural world they create friction so it is true in the interpersonal world of humanity. Any community provides ample opportunity to develop and refine relational skills. It is a well attested view in educational circles that any learning is best done in a meaningful context. We seek to find real-life situations in which to frame Maths problems and we would always seek to undertake scientific experiments in an arena that has purpose. So why when it comes to the development of social and emotional skills would we want to pull the learning out of its context and put it in a series of lessons on a Wednesday afternoon? For one, it does not seem to make good pedagogical sense to me, as the learning loses all sense of contextual background but secondly it is not how anyone learns about relationships in the real world.

Relationships by their very nature are organic and dynamic and occur naturally throughout life. I don't need formal lessons on how to relate to people I just need to find someone, work with them and I will learn all I need to about the way people tick. All of us who are married know that our greatest emotional teacher is our partner. I was not taught in any lesson or any course I have ever been on that the answer to "Does my bum look big in this?" is always "No". I have also learnt that a statement such as "Shall I wear the Blue dress or the Red one?" may sound like a question and may even look like a question when it is written down with its question mark at the end. However, to seek to answer the question with the word "Blue" is a bit like a marital version of Russian roulette because whilst you might guess the right colour I have learnt that the rules of the game are to guess which one my wife has already decided to wear and for which she is simply seeking your affirmation. I have learnt that "I don't know, what do you think?" is the type of answer that allows us to go out holding hands rather than driving to the dinner party in separate cars. Now I am not decrying marriage courses that may exist but surely the most effective way to learn about relationships is to be in one and to learn from it.

So why do we think that taking social and emotional learning out of any context and teaching it as a set of de-contextualised principles is a good idea? I know one might point out that many visit marriage counsellors and this is true but this does not alter the fact that these sessions often focus on the contextual elements the couple are struggling with. In this sense they are more akin to the teacher resolving the disagreement on the playground as opposed to the generic lesson where we all "learn" relational principles.

If we are to do the teaching of relational skills any justice at all we need to remain on the macro scale and look at how the school as a whole community and as a relational entity in and of itself can be subsumed within a social and emotional framework. What we need to create is a curriculum (as they have in other countries) that has the social and emotional element running all the way through it like lettering in a stick of rock. I have never sought to hide the fact that The Wyche Curriculum has this at its heart. The emphasis on "Managing Self" and "Managing Others" are pure relational teaching but the importance of them is that they lie at the heart of what the school seeks to achieve on a daily basis. These elements are woven into every area of the curriculum and subsume all we seek to achieve here at the school. There are no SEAL lessons because every lesson has the potential to be an arena for social learning. Every curriculum project in every class is always undertaken in groups and this in turn provides ample opportunity for relational issues to surface and be dealt with in the context of any lesson. To this end the social and emotional learning is interwoven into the warp and weft of the whole curriculum.

The elements of social and emotional learning are not a class based activity, Instead they should be subsumed in the culture and ethos of the school. The teaching is infused through every aspect of the curriculum whether that is within the formal curriculum taught in lessons or in the informal settings of playtime and other unstructured times. Stating the obvious this calls for a secure whole school approach but it allows the teaching of children and the relational framework it is set within to work seamlessly together.

My own thinking in this regard was shaped by a lesson some time ago when there had been a major fall out in the football game at lunchtime. It involved so many children that I took the opportunity to address the issue as a whole class. It became a spontaneous lesson and lasted most of the afternoon. The two sides involved in the dispute articulated their views and the rest of the class who were not involved were able to feed objective opinions into the debate and take it forward. The whole class were engaged and the discussion ended amicably and successfully but also taught all children relational principles along the way. I remember thinking at the time, that this is the only way to teach such skills in a meaningful context. It would have been crazy to say to the children; "Well don't worry in week 4 of Unit 2 we will be looking at conflict resolution." I know most teachers would take the opportunity to address such issues in a class setting; the difference I would wish to draw out is that the school has no other form of social and emotional teaching, it is all done in this context and is not one aspect of a larger formal programme that runs alongside it.

In operating in this way the key is for teachers to see the opportunities for emotional teaching and pursue them when they arise. I often tell of a time I was in a class at the end of the morning. The children were receiving feedback from the mini-projects they had undertaken throughout the morning. This involved three activities which the children undertook in three different groups, each activity was judged for quality and the winning groups celebrated. The teacher was giving out the awards. As she concluded she suddenly noticed Gemma had been in each of the winning groups and pointed this out to the class. Gemma was given an additional round of applause and the children went out to play. Hang on... stop right there... Why was Gemma in all three groups? What qualities and attributes does Gemma have that allow her group always to flourish? These aspects are often hidden from children (and from adults for that matter!) but need to be drawn out and taught explicitly. This was an opportunity lost in my opinion and was one we were able to correct when the children returned in the afternoon, but it demonstrated to me that if schools want to make deep inroads in this area they need to be always alert to every opportunity to "teach" social skills when a meaningful context arises.

Sadly despite the substantial amount of investment in programmes like SEAL, especially from national government, the research that has sought to analyse its effectiveness has been less than encouraging. The government's own evaluation report stated that: "in terms of impact, our analysis of pupil-level outcome data indicated that SEAL failed to impact significantly upon pupils' social and emotional skills, general mental health difficulties, pro-social behaviour or behaviour problems." Without wishing to labour the point this could simply be down to the fact that de-contextualised learning of any sort will not deliver the desired impact. Whilst this could be said of any individual curriculum subject it is especially true of an all-encompassing aspect of the curriculum such as emotional intelligence.

Conversely Katherine Weare from Southampton University undertook a research report on behalf of the DfE entitled: "What works in developing children's emotional and social competence" She drew the following conclusion; "There is evidence that the school environment is the largest determinant of the level of emotional and social competence and wellbeing in pupils and teachers." Loosed from the requirement to simply look at the impact of SEAL itself Weare's work took in a greater breadth and her conclusion dovetails into those I have expressed; namely that it is only when the social and emotional curriculum is set firmly in the heart of a school's everyday curriculum that any meaningful impact is delivered to the children.

LESSON OBSERVATIONS
HOW CAN WE HAVE GOT IT SO WRONG?

Preface

There are aspects of the educational landscape that are firmly set within a national framework. Many would hold to the view that oft times this is advantageous, there are those who would contend that the introduction of the national curriculum has brought a sense of necessary cohesion. However there have been some elements of the macro framework which have distorted the purity of educational philosophy. For me lesson observations are a prime example of such a malaise and we are now saddled with the concept of the senior leader at the back of the room with their clipboard making judgements from a snapshot of a teacher's lesson. How have we got to such a state?

The Nationally/Macro Situation

Lesson observations were introduced by OFSTED as a means of observing teaching and seeking to gauge its quality. It is as crude a way of measuring the quality of a teacher. In scope it is similar to arriving at a football match at half time and attempting to judge the quality of the players. It leads to rushed decisions often founded on preconceived data such as; this team is winning 2-0 so they must be better, or this player must be good because he has scored both goals. But what about the fact that both goals were tap- ins after some incredible work by the winger who set them both up? Or the goalkeeper, an unsung hero, who made a string of excellent saves to keep his team in the game? Any process becomes data driven when that is all the information people have when arriving cold to a situation. To this end the observation often becomes a means of interpreting the data rather than making a secure, qualitative decision on the true quality of play. Even if you stayed on and watched 10 minutes of the second half it is unlikely that your judgement would be any more secure.   What if the brilliant, dazzling winger of the first half pulled a muscle walking down the tunnel at half time what would the inspector make of his second-half performance? Special Measures one assumes?

But for some reason schools have got into the habit of treating the one-off lesson observation as the panacea of all educational judgement, and that upon it we are able to assess the complete effectiveness of a teacher and their professional expertise. This concept has to be flawed.

The only sympathy I have with Ofsted is that I cannot think of another way of "externally" verifying teaching. So whilst the model is flawed they use it because it is the only considered option at present. So too with LA lesson observations. Their relationship with the school, whilst more supportive that the Ofsted team, is still external and so they come in and monitor using similar externally based procedures which is completely understandable. This is not a direct criticism of either group just an acknowledgement that their role in seeking to effectively monitor or indeed move teaching and learning forwards is hamstrung by the simple fact that their starting point is one of externality and therefore both their knowledge and their influence is limited.

The Local/Micro Mistake

The tragedy is that all too often schools at a local level have used these models of lesson observation as a tool to measure and assess the quality of their own teachers, as if they themselves were external stakeholders. My guess is that they have been driven down this route by two factors.

Firstly they know Ofsted will assess the school in this manner and so there is a subliminal message that is taken on board that if Ofsted use this approach then it must be the accepted and correct way to do things. This rather misses the point – the point is it may well be the "right way" for an external evaluation, although I would argue that the wording should be "it is the only known way". I am minded of Churchill's assessment of democracy, when he said "No one pretends that democracy is perfect or all-wise. Indeed, it has been said that democracy is the worst form of government except all those other forms that have been tried from time to time." So too with external lesson observations it is a crass way to assess the quality of teaching but is simply better than anything else that anyone can think of at present. We have to accept that such an approach is a poor shadow and imitation of what schools should be doing locally.

Secondly there is the understanding that schools will be asked to sit in on lessons with the inspector and assess staff using this rather blunt instrument. This has led to many schools adopting this as "good practice" which it plainly isn't, on the basis that they will need to have had experience of the process before the inspectors arrive at their door. There is wisdom in being prepared for the eventuality of the Ofsted inspection of course, especially for those new to headship but sadly it has driven the idea that this is the "right way" to assess teachers even deeper into schools and into the psyche of senior management teams.

Hence schools have often set up a series of one off lessons and seek to provide feedback to teachers on the basis of these stand-alone observed lessons. How ludicrous is that? Would Real Madrid have paid £85 million for Gareth Bale if they had only seen him play for 20 minutes in one FA cup match against a team two divisions below? Yet apparently our expectation is that heads can go into classrooms, assess a teacher's lesson and on the basis of what they have seen tell them whether they (or indeed the specific lesson) are "Outstanding" or "Satisfactory".

Gareth Bale has his good days and his bad days and so do teachers. More importantly those we work with have their good and bad days. In Gareth Bale's case he cannot shine if the keeper for the opposition is having a blinder and saving everything that is thrown at him. In such a scenario the headline "Bale scores another hat trick" might have to be put on hold as it has been influenced not by a lack in own his ability but is simply being surpassed by the ability of those around him. So too in teaching the learning will splutter and stall if there has been a fall out within the class between groups of children at lunchtime yet we all know that good teachers will shelve lessons and deal with the social and emotional well-being of children rather than seeking to plough on in a vain attempt to demonstrate "expected progress within the following Maths lesson"

This is exacerbated by the fact that the standards agenda is predicated on the need for children to be making continual progress. This has been extrapolated into a form of thinking whereby teachers should apparently be able to demonstrate that the children have made progress within a single lesson or even within a segment of a lesson. I appreciate that if you are monitoring externally this may well be your only means of calibrating the quality of teaching with progress made but to pretend that this is how children learn and that every 20 minutes they should be taking on new concepts with no opportunities to consolidate, apply their learning into fresh contexts or to grapple with concepts that are deep in complexity, is complete nonsense. As Mick Waters has said on many occasions; we all know that children grow in fits and spurts and that their physical growth is not uniformly linear. If we accept that this is the way life is in the physical realm then why can we not accept that it should be any different in the mental realm? The truth is that this is the way learning is, children rarely make uniform progress and yet they all get those light bulb moments (as indeed we do as adults) when the learning spikes as a concept clicks into place for the first time.

The real problem with the current lesson observation regime is that it allows teachers to dust off their "Oscar winning lesson" (as one of my LA inspectors once described them) and dazzle in a lessons lasting less than an hour. This is then followed by an unwitting member of the senior management team seeking to grapple with the task of attaching an Ofsted grade to it, as if this were a cogent way forward in assessing the quality of any teacher.

The reality is that the "outstanding teacher" in the Maths lesson, with one set of children may turn into a "good teacher" when teaching Maths to different set of children and even become "Satisfactory" teaching Ballet in PE. As I have proved to my cost on numerous occasions I can at any time and within any lesson, deliver a piece of learning that is so infused with incompetence that not even the word "unsatisfactory" would adequately describe it.

The truth is that "outstanding teachers" are not those that just deliver "outstanding lessons" though they may well do so, they are those that are "outstanding" in the fullest orb of the professional sense. To make judgements on a single lesson is such a narrow view of what makes a good teacher as to be palpably laughable.

I was walking through the hall the other day which was empty apart from a child sobbing uncontrollably. She was sitting on the lap of one of my female teachers. As I sought to discretely pass by I noted that the discussion hinged on a tragic family situation but more importantly I observed a tear in the eye of the teacher. It takes a special person with a large heart to share in true heart-felt empathy such a moment with a child. I'm not sure what the lesson was after break, I am not sure that if I had monitored it whether I would have observed progress in multiplying fractions, or even whether that progress would have been tangible after 20 minutes but what I do know is that in 20 years' time that child will remember the time that an "outstanding teacher" took the time and trouble to give up her break time to comfort someone in their hour of need.

Just as there is no such thing as a "level 3 piece of writing" there are only level 3 writers, so too there should be no such thing (at a local level) as an "outstanding lesson". The same principle applies, we don't look at one piece of writing and gauge a child's entire writing ability on the evidence of that one piece of work. So too we shouldn't judge teachers on the basis of a single lesson, which in truth is only one aspect of what makes a teacher outstanding. We all know that the best teachers are those who give above and beyond, they play football with children at lunchtime, they run clubs after school, they take interest (or sometimes feign interest!) in those areas of life that children are excited about and as we have said they sit them on their knee and offer deep comfort when their hearts are broken. They will of course be the type of teachers that children warm to and respond well to and their lessons will probably, as a consequence, find the children respectful in terms of behaviour and engaged in terms of learning, but we must not reduce teaching down to the "children's ability to grasp cognitive concepts in as short a time as possible" This can become the driving force behind the "standards agenda" and as I have said to the staff here on many occasions "Children are not just brains on legs" they are human beings in all the fullness that human nature brings.

Local/Micro Lesson Observations

So is there no place for lesson observations in a local school? One of the huge changes in my teaching career has been the access to classes for inspectors and senior leadership teams within schools. I began teaching in a pre-Ofsted era when no-one entered my classroom from one year to the next. I don't believe my teaching was richer because of that and I don't believe returning to these days is a way forward. Interestingly Ofsted have noted that there is often a wider differential in quality within a single given school than between two different schools. The implication of this finding is that most schools have the expertise within themselves to close the gap between its strongest and weakest teachers but are not availing themselves of a solution that lies within their own institution. Therefore we need more collaboration within schools not less and we need to develop a framework where this can flourish. The primary purpose of the lesson observation at a local level should not be for the senior management team to grade the teacher but for them to gain a sense of where the school needs to move forward generically. This may relate to a curriculum area e.g. Maths, or even narrowed down to a single aspect of a curriculum area e.g. Fractions in Maths. Similarly it may be that there are areas of general teaching and learning which should be addressed e.g. the lack of reasoning and dialogue in lessons, or areas of behaviour and management that could be addressed across the school.

The lesson observations are a crucial part of this but teachers should become more comfortable with that fact that senior managers observe their classes, not with a view to feeding back to them personally. It may be true that on occasions the teacher may request help in a given area, or the observer may offer advice on a specific teaching strategy but in all this the greater picture must not be lost which is that this is more a process for whole school development rather than individual teacher assessment. For the former it becomes a very powerful tool to move a whole school forward, for the latter it is a very blunt instrument that is barely fit for purpose.

However it is the continuity and progression that such development brings across the school which is the vital element. Without a shadow of a doubt the schools that demonstrate exemplary progress in their children's attainment are those that have cohesive teaching and learning policies throughout the school as a whole and sustained lesson observations are a crucial factor in data gathering to reach this end.

This turns the lesson observation process on its head. It might make more sense for the teacher to choose to deliver lessons where they are aware of their professional weaknesses when being observed by senior management. If the emphasis switches from the grading of teachers into an unwritten league table and instead focuses on whole school professional development then this would indeed be a cogent way forward. Why do teachers want to be told they have taught an outstanding Maths lesson, when they (and probably the staff appraising them) are fully cognisant of the fact that the teacher has a weakness in the teaching of Art and Design?

We need desperately to shift the ethos of lesson observation heavily towards development and professional support and away from a scenario where every teacher tries to "pass the observation test with flying colours". I knew we had reached a point close to that here at The Wyche when one teacher came to me one day and said; "I am teaching DT tomorrow and I'm rubbish at it can you come and watch?" Why not? What better basis can there be for professional development than a member of staff self-evaluating their own performance (and assessing it accurately!) and then going on to build in their own support structures through a strategic lesson observation by the Headteacher. If we could breed this culture of openness through all our schools what an impact there would be on collaborative learning amongst staff and consequently a rise in the quality of teaching delivered to children.

Conclusion

What I am arguing is that there should be a clear demarcation between the lesson observations undertaken by the external inspector and those used to internally drive a school forward by the senior management team. Inspectors undertake a forensic analysis of a school and deliver a snapshot verdict to the school of its strengths and weaknesses in the form of an audit approach. This is a process that is primarily pragmatically driven because Ofsted does not have time to spend a concerted amount of time in any given school. In that sense it does what it says on the tin and "inspects" the school. Whilst the form of lesson observation it uses may be considered to be deeply flawed they have been developed in response to the constraints they find themselves within.

What I would wish to underscore is that to apply this cut and dried model as a means for leading a school forward is no way forward at all. We need to develop another complimentary framework, which in one sense is the very antithesis of the Ofsted model. This should have as its starting point the long term needs of the school and should be founded on the basis of corporate on-going teacher development rather than an instrument to judge and grade individual teachers on the basis of a single lesson.

The Ofsted emphasis has the feel of a driving test with the ultimate end goal being; Have I passed? The internal framework should remove this completely and should simply pose the question for both the teacher and the school leader – How does what we learnt from this lesson contribute to the on-going process of whole staff development within the school?

Note to Reader: Competency Procedures
I appreciate that all of the above relates to teachers who are outside the remit of competency procedures and I readily accept that this strand of professional development has its own unique set of criteria that need to be followed and adhered to.

Postscript
Whilst this article has addressed the issue of external evaluation through Ofsted I thought it only fair to point out that since writing this document they have produced some excellent guidance on the subject of lesson

observations. There is an acknowledgement on their part, with which most of us would concur that to make a judgement on the quality of teaching based on a single lesson is too limiting and therefore each lesson is to be seen in the context of both the learning of the children and in the quality of learning within the school as a whole Therefore I both welcome and commend to you the thoughts of Mike Chadingbowl, Ofsted's National Director of Schools which he spells out in his document "Why do Ofsted inspectors observe individual lessons and how do they evaluate teaching in schools?"

EPLILOGUE - *WYCHUMVI*

If you have managed to reach this point in the book then may I commend you on your tenacity! Unless of course you are one of those people who always reads the last pages to find out "how the story ends" but then that is just plain cheating!

I trust you found some of the educational thinking behind this eclectic assortment of articles beneficial but as you will be aware this book was not written with the sole purpose of sharing pedagogy. Its primary purpose was to raise funds for Wychumvi, the school's charity. It seems appropriate therefore to conclude the book sharing briefly with you how the money you gave will assist the lives of children in Tanzania.

Wychumvi was established by the Wyche School in 2008 following our first visit to our link school Gofu Juu, in the city of Tanga. The school had many orphans, up to 170 at that time and many of these had no extended family to support them. They were fed from a meagre bowl of watery maize mix and this would often be their only form of sustenance in any given day. Wychumvi was set up to provide a programme to feed these children. Today, some seven years later, we feed a mug of Ugi (a maize based porage) to over 1,000 pupils at the school. We also provide free fruit to replicate the provision our Key Stage 1 children have in this country.

The charity also funded the building of a fence which enabled the school to cultivate a thriving garden producing vegetables that are sold into the community. The money raised is then used to purchase milk to supplement the Ugi programme. This is provided at cost price by Tanga Fresh, a local dairy that supports our work.

In 2011 we raised nearly £2,000 which funded a kitchen. This has enabled us to provide more substantial meals based on maize and beans. These are currently provided twice a week.

At present Secondary education in Tanzania is not free and this precludes those children unable to pay. So in 2012 we established a sister charity called "Wychumvi+" The principle was to link families here in the UK with a child from Gofu Juu with a view to supporting them through their Secondary education. Each sponsor contributes £50p.a. which covers the cost of fees and other items the children require.

In 2013 I was invited to Coventry University where I met with the Dean to look at the possibility of Engineering Undergraduates working in Gofu Juu. So having visited in the summer of 2014 three students returned the following year with funding to build a water harvesting system for the garden as well as building toilet blocks for both children and the staff.

Each day Tanzanian parents find themselves forced to choose between the short term goal of food for today or the longer term goal of education which is the only chance their children have of being released from the poverty trap. The impact of the meals should be evident to all. They offer nutrition to those who struggle daily with hunger and at the same time maintain a continuity of education for every child. Exams results have rocketed not just due to increased attendance but also because concentration and focus in class has improved markedly. It is hard to underestimate the power that the Ugi programme is having upon the lives of so many. Therefore on behalf of all those at Gofu Juu, may I thank you for supporting this work.

Printed in Great Britain
by Amazon

11867342R00140